Blue, Green and Gold

A Clear Path for Crafting a Personal Blueprint for Greener Pastures in Your Golden Years

Michael Steinhardt CLU, ChFC, AIF, CPFA

Copyright © 2020 Michael Steinhardt

All rights reserved. No part of this book may be used or reproduced in any manner whatsoever without prior written consent of the authors, except as provided by the United States of America copyright law.

Published by Best Seller Publishing®, Pasadena, CA
Best Seller Publishing® is a registered trademark
Printed in the United States of America.
ISBN: 978-1-949535-74-7

This publication is designed to provide accurate and authoritative information with regard to the subject matter covered. It is sold with the understanding that the publisher is not engaged in rendering legal, accounting, or other professional advice. If legal advice or other expert assistance is required, the services of a competent professional should be sought. The opinions expressed by the authors in this book are not endorsed by Best Seller Publishing® and are the sole responsibility of the author rendering the opinion.

For more information, please write:
Best Seller Publishing®
253 N. San Gabriel Blvd, Unit B
Pasadena, CA 91107
or call 1(626) 765 9750
Visit us online at: www.BestSellerPublishing.org

Contents

Disclaimer & Advisory iv
Acknowledgments..1
Chapter 1: Defining the Problems and Challenges............................3
Chapter 2: Swimming Upstream 9
Chapter 3: Media Journalism and Agendas.....................................21
Chapter 4: Time 35
Chapter 5: Insurance 45
Chapter 6: Savings 63
Chapter 7: Investing in Equity Markets and
 Historical Perspective 77
Chapter 8: Just Sign Up...99
Chapter 9: DIY, Robo or Advisor? 111
Chapter 10: Why We Work 129
Chapter 11: Story Time and Do's and Don'ts................................135
Appendix: Action Items 141

Disclaimer & Advisory

This material was created to provide accurate and reliable information on the subjects covered but should not be regarded as a complete analysis of these subjects. It is not intended to provide specific legal, tax or other professional advice. The services of an appropriate professional should be sought regarding your individual situation.

All illustrations are hypothetical, and there is no guarantee that similar results can be achieved. If fees had been reflected, the return would have been less.

Although there is some element of building from chapter to chapter, the reader can choose to select chapters to read (out of order) and still get the message being delivered on that particular area.

Securities offered through Kestra Investment Services, LLC (Kestra IS), a member FINRA/SIPC. Investment Advisory Services offered through Kestra Advisory Services, LLC (Kestra AS), an affiliate of Kestra IS. Kestra IS and Kestra AS are not affiliated with Clear Path Advisory, Inc.

Acknowledgments

This is a culmination of a lifetime's work. In no particular order, I want to thank many who have supported me and my career over my three-plus decades in the industry. I want to thank my first set of clients who had trust and confidence in me while I was still in school. Thank you to; Rob Leikin (my very first client); and early clients Steve Rosen, Stuart Title, Kenny Venick, Jon Kramer, Michael Richman, and Scott Robinson for trusting me when I started my career. Thank you to my brother, Paul, for not only his trust and confidence when I started but for also all the other support you have shown over the years. You have been very generous over the years, and I'm appreciative of that. I want to thank my parents, Tom and Barbara, for their love, support, and sacrifices they made in giving me the opportunities I had, and for the love they give to their grandkids. I learned many of life's lessons in watching and observing you both.

I also want to acknowledge anonymously the handful of people that did not do business with me or left me at some point. Although it may sound odd thanking this group, I learned some valuable lessons from the painful moments of loss and failure that surely shaped me and my disposition.

I want to thank all the people that *did* elect to do business with me. For putting your trust and confidence in me, I am humbled and honored. I have been enriched by each and every client relationship. I thank and acknowledge a small circle of close friends who trusted my guidance. Doing business with friends can be uncomfortable for some, so I appreciate that you took that leap of faith and got past the "not doing business with a friend" feeling.

I would like to thank my network of peers, mentors and teachers that have been there for me over the years. The first I want to mention is Bob Walsh, my first general agent when I came into the business. Bob was instrumental in my learning curve early on. He is sadly no longer with us. To David Berman (and his firm) and Fred Shapiro (and his company) in particular, who have been both great friends and sources of inspiration and mentorship. Not sure where I would be today without them. Thank you to Jeff Levy and Mark Kauffman for their friendship and professional relationship we have developed. Thank you, Doug Sandler, for pushing me to complete this book. Thank you to Jeff Friedman and Susan Aronoff for your input and feedback on the book. To some of my study group peers for help along the way, thank you Jo Ann Favia, Tim Corle, Tim Elsworth, James Studinger, Rob Allen, and Steve Hein.

I also want to acknowledge my office staff, my daytime family of Barbara Owens, Lisa Hergenhan and Linda Tarnalicki. We have shared so many moments and emotions that I can't begin to describe. All three have been dedicated, caring, and supportive in their roles and have given me and the clients the best they have to offer. You all have made coming to work an absolute joy each and every day.

Most importantly, I want to also thank my beautiful wife, Jenn, for many things… for being there, for giving me the space to grow, for setting me straight when I would veer off track, for being a great partner and a great mom. You are one of the hardest working people I know, a great example for our kids.

And lastly, to my kids, Tyler and Gabby: thank you for being an inspiration. I have tremendous respect for you both, and I've said often, "I look up to my kids." I love you both dearly and hope there are pearls of wisdom in these pages that will not only benefit you but also your many friends that I've met over the years.

CHAPTER 1

Defining the Problems and Challenges

"No problem of human destiny is beyond human beings."

John F. Kennedy

Let's start this book with the end, the very end, which is the primary goal of this book: the ending ends with you having your monies outlive you. That is it. Plain and simple. If you outlive your money, then something's gone wrong.

When it comes to building our financial security, we logically know when the start is, but we seem to delay getting it going; we take on the task halfheartedly and consistently make decisions counter to our long-term goals. The aim here is to point out the clear path ahead and to get you on a better road to your desired destination and get you there sooner.

Along the road, you will encounter many challenges unforeseen reefs and distractions from endless sources. We will explore the landscape and venues of those places that offer guidance, opinion, and information. This book will help you separate what applies to you and what is just noise.

GPS for Your Retirement Accumulation

What if your retirement accumulation plan was like your car's GPS system? You punch in the location and you are guided to your destination. But what if you go off course? The system automatically readjusts and changes the route based on where you are now. Wouldn't that be great if we had that in our accumulation plan? Each morning or each year, you plug in your retirement GPS and it tells you if you have gone off course and how to get back on track.

For example, if your destination is 30 miles away, but you went off course, the GPS might show you are now 33 miles away. If your dollar-goal for retirement was set at a certain number, but along the way your debt increased, your financial GPS should warn you that you are further from your destination than planned. But in real life, we don't readily see that. We just keep going about our business, living our lives, and veering further off course.

One decision you will have to make is how to go about this journey: do you do it alone or do you use some sort of navigation? Do you pay the cost for said guidance or the cost of not taking advice? We will discuss these choices. There is a role that the advisor plays that could be the fine line between success and failure. In our GPS analogy, think of the advisor as part of that tool. If you didn't have that relationship when you veered off course, would you know or even recognize you are further away?

Stories, Vignettes and Client Examples

One of the ways I try to get across a point is to tell stories (as you can already see) that offer comparisons and paint pictures. I believe we often better see the landscape through storytelling. This topic is littered with statistics and numbers, and we will have to dig into some of those figures, but I'll try not to get buried in them. The idea is to get across concepts and lessons using other methods than the traditional showing of the hard facts.

Saving, protecting, and investing seem very simple. And going on this journey alone will present many challenges. It will be easier to "groove" bad habits (spending too much, going into debt, not saving enough, not protecting elements that need attention and many more) than it will be to instill good habits.

The Landscape When I Started

When I started in the industry in the mid-1980s, the landscape was different. Like many industries, change is inevitable. The shifts in the economy, consumption, living, health and more has had a ripple effect on both related and unrelated industries. Today, then, we have many choices in where and how we spend our money, and this has had an undeniably adverse effect on savings and accumulation. There are so many sources of both information and misinformation that this too makes an impact on the consumer.

The first step is to understand the problem holistically. The big picture. We can learn from the past, but we also need to pivot beyond what was. We will address what previous generations before us were looking at and what *we* need to focus on. These are different challenges and we must tackle them with a different philosophy. What was part of retirement planning a generation ago may no longer apply today.

I read somewhere that it's a possibility that someone alive today will live to 150 years old. The sheer thought of that is crazy, but take that a bit further and consider how many decades of retirement planning that person will need to do in their finite working years to cover their non-working years. It doesn't matter that this may not play out now; what does matter is the progression of our lives is certainly pointed towards living longer. We will take a hard look at that and what it means.

Preview

The next few chapters will address some of the problems that lie ahead.

- **Financial journalism** will play a big part if you allow it to. There is a counterculture to what the financial press says and promotes and what your individual goals are, so we will explore this with examples and suggestions on how to handle this large and growing segment. We can't hide from it, as there is so much out there in so many formats.

- **How the current is running against you**. I will present some interesting and creative thoughts about how certain elements adversely affect your long-term accumulation. By being aware of some of these points, you may act differently.

- **Where time fits in to the equation**. Many of your years may be behind you, so you will have to make some difficult choices about lifestyle and work. If you squandered some of the years "doing what is right," then getting on track may require you to do something different. I'll show you how to find the pockets in your financial life where you can make an impact and start now to better secure your future. There is no right destination but there are greener pastures that we all can strive for, but it will most likely call for change and action. If you have not addressed your financial future to date, then the enemy is clearly, "status quo" and inaction. The solutions won't just happen out of nowhere. You will have to take the lead.

- **Products will play an important part to solving problems**, so we will spend some time talking about the broad solutions. We will touch upon certain lines of insurances, as well as savings and some creative strategies. We will round out the commodities section with investing, investments and offer up an historical perspective. This section will mainly focus on investing in equity markets so we can explore where and why these fit into your equation. Much is said and written about this arena, and there is a lot to decipher, so that is where much of our attention will be focused.

I will make this point several times throughout the book: books have been written on several of these topics alone, so the objective here is not to take a deep-dive into every single aspect but to cover sufficient ground to motivate you to make better choices. I don't claim to be the smartest guy in the room, but my life's work is centered around making my clients' lives better by helping them make stronger decisions. Oftentimes, the reward of that work is years down the road, so it's hard for clients to see the advantages in the moment. However, the alternative to this delayed gratification is consuming and spending, which the consumer is fighting to resist. One of the messages in these pages is to act differently. This is not to say, we can't consume and spend money (we can and we should), but we also need to properly place that element in our lives and address what our future holds for the current trajectory versus if we make changes.

The final chapters will open the discussion of an element that is important and yet so simple to grasp. We will compare and contrast how to go about having sustainable dollars in our golden years. You will hopefully end this book feeling motivated to get on a better path towards financial independence and to see more clearly the landscape ahead.

There Are Solutions

Recognizing the problem first and foremost is critical. Then making the necessary changes going forward is next. Sounds simple, but never easy. Common sense will reign, but execution will be the challenge.

We must face the problem and how best to solve it. The problem is having sustainable income for all of our years. Imagine if I told you, the success of your plan was at a 70% rate? Would you accept those rates if you were having surgery? Would you accept those rates from an airline that told you that was the chance of reaching your destination? No? So, why are you settling for a less than success rate for your retirement? This is one element we have some layer of control over.

We don't get to choose a lot in life, but we can work towards defining our golden years in the fashion we imagine. That is what much of this book will be about, to finding ways to build that sustainable wealth, so your money can outlast you.

My motivation was to touch more lives, and this medium allows me to connect with you, without being in front of you. I hope there are nuggets contained within these pages that help you. From time to time, I get direct feedback from a client about the work I did and the difference it made for them. And I will admit, it's intoxicating. It's fuel for me, and it validates the role I play and confirms this was my calling: to make a difference in other peoples' lives. Now, I am excited to make a difference in your life, so, let's get into it.

Action Items:

- Grab a note pad or highlighter, and when something is stated that hits home, jot it down or highlight it. Reflect upon your situation and think about what changes you can make.
- Think about your current retirement plan. Is your trajectory one you are proud of or does it need attention?

CHAPTER 2

Swimming Upstream

"Dreams will not be thwarted; faith will be rewarded."

Bruce Springsteen, "Land of Hope and Dreams"

Salmon are born in fresh water and then migrate to a river to live for a few years. But to spawn, they swim upstream to a similar location of their birth to lay their eggs. Sadly, that journey will often result in their demise after spawning.

In my more than three decades in the industry, I have seen that we seem to mimic this behavior of swimming upstream with our financial decision-making—meaning, we make it more difficult for ourselves time and time again.

Because of our behavior as consumers and investors, I believe we are more prone to financial failure than success. Human nature, being what it is, drives us to results that are lacking in the arenas of protecting, savings, and investing. Like several of the other habits we battle with, financial success is dependent upon sound decision-making, long-term planning, "stick-tuiativeness," and discipline.

Bad habits are easier to groove then good habits. It is much easier to eat junk food than it is to eat healthily. It is much easier to not exercise than to be disciplined and exercise. And it is much easier to spend money now than save for your future.

This chapter, we will look at some of the many scenarios we (as investors and consumers) come face to face with. The list is long. The current is strong and, of course, it is against us. Most of us are not born into a life of financial independence; we must earn, save, and accumulate wealth. Only a select few are, as the expression goes, "starting life on third base," but didn't hit a triple to get there.

As we start our working lives, the following issues are not remotely close to what we would deem important. Most likely, we are too busy learning new skills, crafts, systems, environments, people and more. We are not yet interested on the tail end of our working career because we just got started! And what happens is, we start forming habits of earning and then spending what we make (and sometimes above what we make). And before we know it, a decade or two of our working lives has passed us by and we failed to pay attention to our long-term picture. Too often we are too busy to be aware there are problems, so the idea here is to start recognizing the issues sooner, allow us time to alter our behavior, which in turn will lead to better results. So, let's dive in and get started.

Here is a list of some reasons and scenarios that, as investors, we tend to fall short in building the wealth we so strongly desire (in no particular order):

> **We start (too) late and want to retire too soon.** We are starting to take retirement planning seriously in our forties and fifties, not in our late twenties or early thirties. These early years are critical to compounding, which we will expand upon later. We delay the start way too long and don't fully understand the consequences. In addition to starting late, we have the desire to retire at a young age. You are the one who makes the decision as to when you want to stop working and there are many reasons and factors that come into play here, not just financial, but we'll need to have enough resources to

even consider that decision, and we'll need to take into account how long we'll need money to last. Leading us to the next issue.

We are living longer in retirement. Whereas we used to have to plan for a few years' in retirement, now we have to plan for a few decades. Some people are even living as many or more years in retirement than the years they spent working, so starting early becomes hyper critical. We will take a deeper dive in this issue later in the book.

We tend to invest emotionally. We often react to market drops and dips with fear and panic, not according to any plan that was created. Studies have been done that compare what investors earn versus what markets earn. And time and time again, markets outperform investors. The reason for this can be traced to emotions. When markets drop, investors get scared; they panic and then react to these emotions. That reaction is all too often dumping stocks and either buying bonds or going to cash. And when stock markets then rise, the flow of money into them rises. So, essentially investors are getting out when markets drop and plowing money in when markets rise—an action that couldn't be more detrimental. This is arguably the Achilles heel of investors. More on this topic later in the book.

Ease of using a credit card. In addition to being a convenient way to pay for goods and services, a credit card promotes us to spend more. We tend to assign a lower cost when charging whereas, when you use cash, we tend to assign a greater cost. We spend more freely using credit. This often leads to another problem: we are charging more than our ability to pay and so we create a debt problem. We tend not to know our monthly purchase total until we get the bill, and then we can't pay it off in full, and so starts the debt cycle. This leads to not only paying for the item we purchased but also paying interest. The following month, we make more purchases and compound the problem, instead of compounding the solution by adding to your investment portfolio.

Consumption is at a faster pace, and there is a lot more to choose from. Many years ago, people would buy electronics that would last many years. There was no need to update or upgrade them. Today, for example, computer systems last a few years, and we need to update and upgrade them regularly. Consumers want to keep up with that latest technology. You may need greater speed or storage to keep pace, but oftentimes it is a choice and the purchase is out of want, not need.

Our hobbies and passions are also victim to this "throwaway culture." Take golf, for example. It used to be that equipment and accessories lasted years. Today, avid players will upgrade and replace items most every year or two, and the cost of those upgrades has skyrocketed. For example, a driver is upwards to $500. It wasn't that long ago that you could buy a whole set of clubs for that price. Companies and manufactures are designing "better" equipment, while some are just marketing their products to highlight greater value. Consumers are seeking improvement, so they are willing to pay the price every other year or so.

And the abundance of choices today over a generation or two ago is nearly unlimited. For example, there used to be one type and color of jeans; today you can have dressy jeans, jeans of different colors, jeans with holes (those used to be the ones you threw out), faded jeans, low-rise jeans, wide-leg jeans, tight jeans, corduroys and so on.

It used to be there were limited options for certain items; for example, belts and socks. Years ago, there were a few colors, styles and patterns. Today, these accessories have near-endless designs. Why am I pointing this out? A generation or two ago, would have spent a minimal amount of money on items like these. Today, people are spending more of their disposable dollars on such items, leaving them fewer dollars to invest for their long-term needs. These are just a few examples—a tip of the iceberg.

We are spending more, spending faster, recycling at a quicker pace. These are all factors that are counter to long-term savings and investment. And time and time again, we justify our (bad) behavior, yet we don't see the long-term harm we are doing in that moment.

Buying is much easier. It used to be you had to buy items at the store, so the spending hours were limited, and the range of products was also limited by the shelf and floor space. Today, you can shop from home 24/7. Essentially, the stores are always open. And when shopping online, we tend to "browse" into other departments and look at additional items, so our "cart" starts to fill up. Today, online retailers offer an almost unlimited supply of goods, so we can be shopping for one particular item but be tempted to add something unrelated to our cart because it was a click away.

Formerly, a limited number of items could be financed, like a car. Today, you can finance almost any big-ticket item. This makes the larger purchases a lot easier to acquire. This is both good and not so good. Before we know it, our monthly fixed obligations are more than just a mortgage or rent.

Delayed gratification versus the joy and immediacy of consumption. Do you take a $5,000 vacation or add $5,000 to your retirement plan? Which sounds better? Which one can be "delayed"? Would you rather upgrade or update a room in the house or put money towards your "old age"? Most of us have a limited dollar chasing an unlimited want, need or desire, so we often have to make choices in life. We look at the choice between consumption today and socking away dollars for tomorrow, and because tomorrow seems so far off, we perceive that best option as spend now. We convince ourselves we can do both, that we can spend this money now *and* save other monies for our future. Only to find that "then" we have another choice (where we choose to spend versus invest) or we will have that ever-present "life happens" moment that something goes wrong and we don't really have a choice (for example, a repair on the house or car). It just doesn't always work out the way we would wish. Rarely do we feel the kind of joy of investing that we get from consumption.

We underestimate the true cost of retirement and overestimate our ability to resolve it. We are trying to estimate how much we need to invest for decades down the road and how long those dollars need to last (also decades). And we are trying to "budget" for things we can't anticipate but will surely spend money on. Generations before us saved for what their lifestyle was, not what they expected it might be. People in their seventies today are spending money on items like cell phones or various subscriptions that were not around when they were starting to save for their retirement. No fault of theirs; they couldn't have foreseen those needs. We often think we'll spend less in our retirement years, when, quite possibly, we will spend an equal amount or more.

Another example. Wouldn't it be nice if you could afford to take your entire family on a vacation? When you were younger, it was difficult to take major trips; the cost was a burden. But later in life, the thought of taking your entire family (kids, their spouses, grandkids) is something many of us would strongly desire. Something like this will cost a small fortune that we didn't account for prior to retirement. Sometimes, pockets of our retired life might actually cost more than we ever anticipated.

Loss of employer pensions has led to a more difficult road to financial freedom. It used to be, most large companies gave retirement benefits in the form of pension plans, and employees were essentially free to spend and consume all of their take home pay with the luxury of knowing their financial future was being addressed. Today, that is the exception and not the rule. The responsibility has been passed to the employee of funding their own retirement via the most popular retirement plan, the 401(k). A 401(k) plan is really considered a *savings* plan. This concept was unheard of 50 years ago when both pensions and Social Security were sufficient that consumers didn't have to set aside additional monies during their working years. They were free to spend. Consumers today have it the other way. Although they are free to spend (what they have and what they don't have), they need to create wealth from scratch.

No more "jobs for life." Generations ago, people would work for one or two companies during their working lives. Today, we are trending upwards of ten employer relationships in our lives. The effect is devastating in two specific areas:

1. Most companies that sponsor a retirement plan often have a waiting period (most commonly a year), and people often don't take the initiative to invest during that waiting period. If you then multiply that ten times (for the ten companies you may work for), that's a decade of accumulation time lost. Remember, we only have about 40 years of normal working time, so carving out ten years is a reduction of 25%. The loss of these years and the loss of the compounding on the back end is devastating.

2. For the first few job changes, young workers have small retirement account balances and often have various forms of debt (car loans, student loans). They have accumulated a few dollars in their retirement plans, enough to be tempted to cash them out instead of rolling them over to their new plan or an IRA. The thought is, after taxes and penalty, the cash in hand is worth more today than at retirement time 30 to 40 years down the road.

For example, what I often see is someone who has accumulated, say, $8,000 in their first job's 401(k) plan and then leaves that company. Having debt, they realize they can get access to about $5,000 by cashing in when they leave that job to pay off some loans. The common thought here is, "I am young and retirement is decades away and I can make good use of this money." Again, devastating results appear at the back end when those dollars are not available to accumulate and compound. Let's look at another example, say a 35-year-old that has accumulated $30,000 in a 401(k) and leaves Company A. Instead of rolling the monies over to a new plan or IRA (because he might think he's got 30 more years till retirement), he cashes out and buys a new car. His net proceeds after taxes and penalty will be roughly $20,000. What is the cost of that car at retirement is a question very few are asking. Your first answer might be $10,000 of taxes and penalty, but if we project the money to double say every ten years, that $30,000 (the gross amount that would stay invested) turns to $60,000 to $120,000 and lastly $240,000. Essentially, that car today cost his future-self around $200,000. That better be one nice car!

Thinking minimums not maximums. Companies often will offer an incentive to enter their 401(k) plan, like offering 50 cents on the dollar up to 5%. Many people let the tail wag the dog, meaning they will enroll in the plan and defer up to that limit, but no more. No more, because they are not being matched above those limits, so they cut off their long-term accumulation noses to spite their short-term faces. And on top of that, they stay static for years, never bumping up their contributions, as if the 5% were a locked-in number. This form of inertia has lasting negative consequences. The question that begs analyzing is what is the MAXIMUM you can contribute? Start with the plan maximums and work down. For 2020, 401(k) plans allow someone under 50 to contribute $19,500, and if you are over 50 an additional $6,500. SIMPLE plans allow participants to contribute $13,500 plus $3,500 if you are 50 and older. So, evaluate from the top limits as to what you can do. If you can't max-out at $19,500 a year, how about $14,000? The key is not to minimize but maximize. Reminder: this is for you and your future lifestyle. You are not spending more; you are investing more in your future.

Monthly and annual dues/memberships. It used to be when you bought something years ago, that was the cost. Nothing else. Today, when you buy a television, there comes the cost of premium stations. Cell phones have large monthly costs. And if you have multiple devices, then that monthly bill will be higher as service fees for each device (cell phone, iPad, tablets) are added. You have to pay memberships to shop at bulk stores, pay "rights" to buy sports tickets (and then the tickets), pay monthly costs to listen to music, pay fees to monitor your credit, pay for space (both physical in terms of storage units and / or digital in terms of cloud), pay for water (delivery of bottles), many pay a monthly service fee for identity theft, home security systems, home repair services and on and on. These items really add up and cut into your ability to save for your future. We are drowning in these monthly expenses. Individually, they don't seem so bad, but collectively they hurt. As our fixed monthly expenses have skyrocketed so has our ability to accumulate long-term dollars. We pay those other bills that come due, and we minimize our contributions to the 401(k) plans (which we deem optional).

The immediacy of results and information. This oftentimes works against us. We can log into our accounts and check our performance, balances, and results. This often leads to action and reaction. This convenience is a disease more than it is a cure. Easy access to information puts decision-making more in the hands of consumers, who tend to sabotage themselves while trying to do what is best. As Pogo Possum said, "We have met the enemy and he is us." Generations ago, you would get an annual statement for your pension account. You rarely gave it much thought between those statements. Looking at your stock portfolios was often quarter to quarter, or you looked it up in the newspaper in the long list of stock quotes. Today, that information is scrolling across the bottom of TV news feeds and popping up as alerts on our cellular devices, so we are constantly looking. This has led to greater reaction based on emotion, and this has been documented to be detrimental.

Pessimism reigns more heavily than reality. Many investors have a long-term pessimistic view of the markets and the economy. Media has a lot to do with this. There are more negative stories to scare consumers and to keep them "tuned in" (bad news sells). Yet, reality says something different. Life and the world are infinitely better than they're portrayed by the media. We are reducing or eliminating many of the diseases our ancestors perished from and have better access to healthcare than ever. We are reducing hunger around the world. We can travel more efficiently, in greater comfort, at a faster speed ... and we are just getting started. How many more years off will it be before individuals have access to their own flying pods?!

Associating risk and volatility as the same. The real risk consumers fail to see is that they most likely will outlive their money. The risk investors tend to focus on is the short-term (daily) fluctuations of markets. The equity markets, in the long term, have reduced risk; as you look at longer holding periods, the number of "down" years declines. To get those long-term results, we must be in the markets at all times, as no one can predict market movements. It's like taking medicine: it often tastes nasty, even though we know it works. The discipline to stay the course under adverse conditions can be the most difficult element. Understanding our holding period is key. Measured in days, weeks and months, the market can experience steep inclines and declines. But measured over years and decades, these gyrations are "flattened out" and movement you will see on a chart is from the lower left to the upper right—a steady incline. History speaks loud and clear, but risk and volatility are often confused.

A portfolio is not a plan. Many fail to implement a well-thought-out comprehensive plan. Most investors think the act of investing *is* the plan, when it really is just a component of the plan. When a comprehensive plan is present, results tend to favor those individuals to a much greater degree than those that don't take the time and energy to build a plan.

We are helping our parents and kids ... sometimes at the same time. We didn't plan for these expenses, but they are taking from future resources. A drain of tremendous magnitude. We may have to support our kids and elderly parents longer than we bargained for. And, in the case of parents, their failure to fully support themselves is now their kids' problem. That situation then feeds itself in that it limits your ability to fully fund your own retirement.

Education and information are not enough. We live in an age when access to information is in abundance and easily accessible. But having or knowing is not correlating to doing the "right thing." The chasm of knowing and doing is still large. Execution is critical to success. Knowing how to hit a golf ball is wonderful, but actually doing it is very different. Specific to your long-term savings and accumulation, knowing all this information is great. But you must take the necessary steps to execute.

Buying individual stocks is closer to speculating than investing. For most, buying single stocks is a difficult way to go, yet so easy to do and so tempting. Investors often have little information about the company; they only know it by the public name, meaning, they rarely know financial metrics, trends, position in the marketplace and more. Money managers have the tools, insight, information to make decisions, whereas consumers have word of mouth, commercials, and a one-page factsheet about the company. But that's just one issue. Buy a stock, see it rise quickly, then what? Get out? Stay the course? See it fall. Then what? Investors will rarely know why it might rise or fall rapidly, so decision-making gets difficult. To keep this conversation in check here, there is nothing wrong with speculating and trying to take greater risk for potentially faster results, just keep this amount of money at a minimum. There are many outlets here that make it easy for investors to get started (low fees, easy access and information), but in the end, this is not the road to success for the majority. This is best served by using professionals and diversification. (Using diversification as part of your investment strategy neither assures nor guarantees better performance and cannot protect against loss of principal due to changing market conditions.)

As you can see, investors have many challenges to be financially secure. This chapter may be a nice "read," but unless we institute change and the discipline to stick to that change, these words are nothing more than a Sasquatch sighting. Real solutions and financial independence can be achieved, but it will oftentimes take conviction, discipline, a trusted relationship, faith in the future, the desire to forego something today and determination to make it happen. We will best serve ourselves by not sabotaging our financial story, by working with the current, not against it, and by making small, positive changes that yield larger beneficial results.

Action Items:

- List which of the factors described above you have encountered in your life.
- List the factors that you can work to eliminate.
- Which are the top three factors you need to eliminate in your life?

CHAPTER 3

Media Journalism and Agendas

"Human flight in a machine might be evolved by the combined and continuous efforts of mathematicians in from one million to ten million years."

From an article in the New York Times, October 9, 1903 after the Langley brothers failed in their effort to get a vehicle off the ground.

"We started assembly today."

From the diary of the Wright Brothers, October 1903

There used to be a time when you read something it carried weight. If it was published or documented, then it must have been true. Of course, this really wasn't the case all the time, but it felt that way. Or how about if you turned on the television and heard someone offering advice on something, that too must have been right, correct? News anchors of yesteryear were held in high esteem, had strong reputations, and were revered. Today, it seems, there is a great divide motivated by political stance and many news anchors have abused their celebrity to the point that it's hard to trust many.

In this day and age, when information is so abundant and constant, where news is delivered in short snippets, there seems to be an endless supply of opinion on almost any topic, so it is sometimes hard to separate what is useful and what is noise. The same story can be told on two differing sides, but the slant and manipulation of the so-called facts can cause the story to favor one side, and this applies to market news.

No matter how successful, innovative and creative companies are, the media slant seems to come out on the negative side. When the market is up, it's just a matter of time before the other shoe drops!

So, let's see if we can determine what message to listen to and what to discard.

A Client Came to Me with an Article in Hand

One client, who came on board in 2011, was just starting to see an upturn following the drop in the 2007/2008 bear market. He emailed me an article in 2013 that said something about "another bear market was coming and to get out of the market." He wanted to discuss what my thoughts were on the article and what he should do based on what the article was saying to do. Clients often send articles my way to comment on the content and offer an opinion as to what change should be made in their portfolio. Why should an investor do anything, why does an investor that read some random article feel the need to act? Why do we do this to ourselves?

Let me give you a little background about the client here that might help. At that time, he was 48, married, and had two kids. He was behind the curve in terms of retirement accumulation, which he was aware of. He got started late and was sidetracked paying for his kids' education, and he was paying a lot more than anticipated and paying for more years than he expected. (Private school all the way through high school inhibits that ability to save for college. This is a hurdle for many.)

He presented the article as if it were gospel and not wanting to repeat what happened a few years back, in terms of "losing money." He expressed, as the article stated, the market was the problem. And he could do something now before another deep drop came to light.

A phrase that needs attention is "losing money." You see, when markets drop (and they do and they will), we assign the peak of the market as one reference point and the bottom as another and then measure our account value just on those days, so we can then determine a so-called loss. In reality, it's not a loss. Of course, it's a drop. However, you might not have bought the stock at its peak, so your measuring stick is inaccurate. The expression "loss" is the wrong word investors often cling to, when they really mean to say, "The portfolio took a drop for a finite period."

This is not to say financial journalism is wrong, evil, or off base. It depends upon the context. An article could point out, based upon various economic metrics, that difficult times are coming and market slides could happen. That's simply fact, but to then using that to determine what an investor should do is where the danger lies. Do not assign meaning as an investor, when meaning is not being delivered.

Media, Message and Perspective

My aim here is to give you a shield to ward off the onslaught of media information being blasted at you. These messages are not designed for you, they are not customized for your situation, so heed this warning: listening to the majority of what is "out there" is hazardous to your financial well-being (except this book).

The message the media puts out there is optimized for their agenda, which is to keep you tuned in: they want a cliffhanger before the commercial break. But for the long-term patient investor, the movement of the tortoise is uneventful, it is the opposite of exciting. These qualities don't dovetail well with media's desire to attract more attention with a negative slant on financial journalism.

Yet, we (as investors and consumers) tend to crave this information. We want to confirm our beliefs, we want to know what is happening right now and what should we do today. We have trouble seeing the big picture in our instant-results world.

The media wants you to believe that gauging the pulse of the market is critical. Should you stay in or get out? The pulse investors should be monitoring is their own in terms of will their money outlive them. This, my dear friends, is the key element. This is the main focus of every advisor worth his or her salt who is planning your financial future.

Nowhere in the mission statements of news outlets, does it say something like, "We seek to provide valuable, customized information for Rob and Mindi, so they can retire in greater comfort." Their goal, generally speaking, is to sell more papers, sell more subscriptions, have you tune in with them regularly.

As a consumer, you are left to sift through the noise. Determine what is accurate, what is real, what is legitimate, what applies to you, what needs to be discarded and what is just entertainment. Really ANYONE can voice their opinion; so, if you're reading an article and you really don't know who is offering up their opinion, think twice. Would you just take anyone's opinion regarding your health, for example? My advice is do not take just anyone's opinion regarding your financial world.

The Real Problem with My Client

The client who sent me the article and I discussed the REAL problem. The real problem was that he and his partner were heading to retirement time with about 50% of what they wanted, in terms of their current lifestyle. This was a risk they weren't seeing clearly. There was a big gap between how they were living now and how they would live if they kept along that same path.

With roughly two decades left of working and investing, we looked at how they would be affected in the long term WHEN markets did drop. By changing his perspective, he could see that drops were leverage: an upcoming slide in the market was NOT a setback but an opportunity to buy at lower prices. We spent some time talking about investing regularly and how, when investing in those down periods, those dollars worked better in the long run. By seeing how much further the investment went during those dips and drops, my client was able to see more clearly that market tumbles were actually his "friend," not the enemy.

Lastly, I pointed out to my client the "facts" about the market, long term that the article did not mention. We looked at long stretches of the market (over any period), discussed their holding periods, looked over the chart of the last dozen or so "bear markets" (starting from World War II) and what happened after them. He realized the article had nothing to do with him. He recognized the hyperbole and sensationalism being presented. The article was suggesting action when action was not the right move.

What Really Happened

Since I have the luxury of hindsight, that so-called prediction of the upcoming "bear market" that the article warned about never happened. Actually, the opposite happened. The market went up. Not only that year, but the following five out of six years, including 2019, when the market soared in excess of 30%.

But the market going up does not prove my point or validate anything. Had the market dropped, that would not have made the article right either. The problem was not what the market was doing or going to do next. The problem was the client was falling short of their retirement accumulation goal. Investing in vehicles tied to the equity markets were the long-term solution to get them closer to their goals and desires. That is what we needed to keep our eye on.

But then coronavirus happened. The first quarter of 2020, the market has retreated and entered another bear market mostly due to the Covid-19, and at the end of this first quarter of 2020, the outlook in the near term is shaky at best. The economy and the world are on hold, business is being halted, and this will certainly have some adverse effect on the markets and the economy. Unlike other bear markets, this one is certainly taking a different path in terms of how widespread it is affecting the world (not just markets but people). This is uncharted territory. But, as we will later see in the book, markets, people, dreams, aspirations, and drive are resilient. History may prove to be a strong guide.

Again, to the long term, patient investor, this news cycle of market gyrations is irrelevant. What happens this week, this month, even this year has no effect on the long-term investor. That person is seeking to create wealth over a 30-year horizon TO retirement, and then they will have potentially another 30, maybe 40 years IN retirement. So, you think a month's worth of drops will have any bearing 50 years from now?

But the media wants you to believe that it does. They want to put an entertaining spin on it. A tortoise race is not going to fill any stadiums. People want to watch greyhounds or horses race, so the slow and steady race is not worth their attention. But in Aesop's fable of "The Tortoise and the Hare," the hare was beaten by the tortoise because it didn't rush around making mistakes.

In a decades' long venture, the market slides are a good thing. Embrace them. These declines are a natural element that we will see (both in reality and later in this book). Expect them. And, when they do happen, expect financial journalism to opine on what you should do. Beware (ignore) financial journalism. Regular investments during this current bear market in 2020 will prove valuable and enriching when we look at where the markets will be in 2030, 2040 and further out. We are buying at dips during the pandemic. That is not a bad thing at all.

Examples of Articles

I have amassed a collection of articles that offer predictions, analysis, updates and more that I have as reference points. If you were to just read the headlines, you might make meaning from them and take action. Action, that would have been detrimental to your long-term growth and success. But these sources and authors didn't care about that, so be careful what you read. For entertainment purposes, here are some of the articles and a brief description:

- "The Death of Equities." Written in 1979 by Barry Ritholtz and published in *Newsweek*, the article describes how in the 1950s there was a massive promotion by Wall Street that brought in many investors to the stock market. But by the 1970s, there were fewer shareholders and younger people were avoiding stocks. The article went on to say, "For better or worse, then, the US economy probably has to regard the death of equities as near permanent condition – reversible someday, but not too soon." This couldn't be further from reality, in hindsight. It went on to say, "The old rules no longer apply. By buying stocks, investors could beat inflation. People no longer think of stocks as an inflation hedge. We're going to see more investments in diamonds, gold bars, Krugerrands and silver coins." Why, yes, Krugerrands. Seems they have taken off! (Not.) FYI, the S&P 500, at the time the article was written, was 108. In 2019, the S&P 500 broke the 3,000 range. No doubt, this article influenced many people out of equities, when this was not about the "death of equities" at all but closer to a rebirth. And that growth from 1979 to today was a double-digit annualized return. Not too shabby for something that was considered "dead."

- "A Market Forecast That Says 'Take Cover'" by Jeff Sommer (July 3, 2010), was published in the *New York Times*. The article starts out by saying, "The stock market lurching again, plenty of investors are nervous and some are downright bearish." Honestly, I'm not exactly sure what "lurching" means and in what context he's using it. The author goes on to quote someone who said he was "convinced that we have entered a market decline of staggering proportions—perhaps the biggest of 300 years." Wow, now that is a long time. Imagine an investor reading THAT. What do you think they might do? He goes on to say that "even the skeptical investors should take this advice seriously. I'm saying, Winter is coming. Buy a coat. If I'm wrong, you're not hurt. If they are wrong, you're dead. It's pretty benign advice to opt for safety for a while." Again, since I have the luxury of hindsight, let's see what happened since that article. At the time of the article, the Dow Jones was at 9,686. The Dow hit 29,000 in early 2020, although Covid-19 has pushed the Dow back down to the 22,000 range at the end of the first quarter of 2020. Into the second quarter, the Dow has risen above 26,000. So, this author's comment that you are not hurt couldn't be further from the truth, even with this most recent drop. If you got out of the market and invested your money in cash and it didn't grow, would you consider that "not hurt"? The title of the article is giving you "the action item," so what do you think many investors did if they just read the title? For sure, they got scared and got out of the markets. But I repeat, had the market dropped for a period after the article, it's not about the prediction being right in the moment; it's about the long term—what solutions are best to solve YOUR problems. I can't imagine going to "cash" is or was the right answer. And I don't recall seeing a follow up from that author saying his advice was off base or inaccurate.

- "Shell shocked Investors Quit the Market." After a recent downturn, this article appeared in *USA Today* in September 2, 2010. The article talks about how tough it has gotten to make money in the stock market, so investors have lost confidence and are paring back their equity positions and moving to safer investments like cash and bonds (a common suggestion / theme played over and over again). To offer perspective, in the days leading up to that article, the market was off by 9%. On that date of the article, the S&P 500 was at 1,122, but three years after, the S&P 500 stood at 1,687. In 2020, the S&P 500 hit 3,300 only to come back down to 2,600 (and back to over 3,000 in the second quarter of 2020). Financial journalism seems to think that down markets are bad and we should not participate in them. This couldn't be more harmful to the consumer. The irony in this article is the expression "safe investments like cash and bonds"—because, long term, they are not safer at all. They have lower volatility but do no keep pace with the rising cost of goods, so essentially you are assured of running short of money using those as your long-term vehicles.

- "For Millions, 401k Plans Have Fallen Short." This was published on the CNBC website by Kelley Holland, March 29, 2015. She describes the current landscape of the 401(k) as the vehicle for retirement benefits and the shift of responsibility from the employer to the employee. The gist of the article was why 401(k) plans have fallen short, not why *investors* are falling short. Reading this article leads me to believe the problem lies with the product, when in reality it lies within each of us. Yes, society has changed and we need to take responsibility for our own retirement today. But people reading this will have read that its someone else's fault, and then not invest in their own 401(k). Potentially disastrous.

I could write an entire book of pieces I see, articles, blog posts and more. Beware. Better yet, don't read them. The funny thing about people who predict and prognosticate is that, by the law of averages, their doom scenario will play out; when it does, occasionally, they like to remind people, "I called that drop in _____" (fill in a year the market dropped). Of course, they don't tell you the other many times they got it wrong, and they certainly don't retract the poor advice they gave you to get out of the market before the market went up again. Of course not.

And as for those who predict markets, I have never seen any of them on a list of the wealthiest people in the country. If they were so smart and could predict to the extent they espouse, don't you think at least one of them would make someone's rich list?

Just like warning labels on prescription drugs, on cigarettes, on amusement park rides, we need warning labels on many financial articles. "Beware: what you are reading, could be hazardous to your financial wellbeing." Or, "These predictions may or may not come true, so read the article for amusement purposes only." Or, "I'm just offering one opinion, I'm not saying this is right or accurate or it even remotely applies to you." Maybe if financial articles had this at the beginning of the piece, people would properly place credence on the message with less weight. And act less often.

The simple fact that people have a forum to offer their opinion to others doesn't make them "experts" on the topic. Having a pen and paper, having a computer, buying time for an infomercial doesn't mean that what they say or write is accurate, truthful or even beneficial. And it certainly doesn't mean it applies to YOU.

Article on Market Prognosticators

There was an interesting article that came out a few years ago titled "A Visual History of Market Crash Predictions" by Michael Johnston. He examined six individuals and their market prognostications. These weren't just articles, many of these were business interviews on TV or print.

One common element of all of these so-called prognosticators is they are all selling something, from books, to publications to online account memberships. One of them has authored nine books and one of them is titled *Think Astrology and Grow Rich*. So, what many fail to clearly see is these people have their own agenda. I am not saying this is wrong at all, but keep in mind what their goal is (to sell subscriptions) and what their goal is not (to advise you).

Many claim to have predicted some past market drop. Again, keep this in perspective. The broad index has a negative year about a third of the time, so drops are quite normal. Predicting a loss is not uncommon, but using that prediction to "prove" an ability to see future ones is delusional.

In Summary

The premise of this chapter is about the media and the negative onslaught we, as investors and consumers, contend with on a regular basis. A day doesn't go by that someone isn't predicting some doomsday scenario, and investors listen to these people as if they are speaking the gospel. Take a strong, long look at THEIR history and then take a long look at the markets history and determine where you want to put your financial trust: in someone with an agenda (books, seminars, publications to sell) or a financial advisor who is looking out specifically for you and your situation? Please note, this is not to say, markets are perfect and rise in a linear fashion. Not at all, they are not perfect, and they do have hiccups from time to time.

One of beautiful elements of the client story presented earlier is that the client took the time to communicate what he was reading and feeling. He also gave me ample time to drill down and discuss what the information in the article meant to him. In the end, he recognized the article for what it was (and was not) and doubled down his efforts to work hard, reduce spending and debt, and increase his savings and investing. And this is starting to pay dividends, but the real benefit will be years into the future.

Action Items:

- Over the next three months, gather a few pieces from the internet that offer market guidance. Build your own file, so that in a year's time, you can look back and see what might have been detrimental to your long term portfolio. This will allow you to see firsthand that not everything posted or written is the truth or that its advice that is best serving you specifically.

- Look up what the Dow Jones and the S&P 500 indexes were the year you were born. And of course, look up where it is today. And take a moment to bask in how our market has performed in those years. Keep in mind what you are seeing is only the price movement of the index, not the dividend it has paid, so you'll need to take that into account (for example, the S&P has averaged about 2% dividend per year). Even with the so-called bear markets.

- The real action item is to actually remove yourself from reading and listening to the financial pornography. If you can do that, then I strongly believe you will be better off in the long run.

- Consider for a moment in one of our last really deep market "crashes" (2007-2008), what if instead of getting out, you doubled down and got in with more money? If you could, would you have invested more money then? Even at the peak, would you have?

Notes:

The Dow Jones Industrial Average is a popular indicator of the stock market based on the average closing prices of 30 active U.S. stocks representative of the overall economy.

S&P 500 Index is an unmanaged group of securities considered to be representative of the stock market in general. You cannot directly invest in the index.

CHAPTER 4

Time

"It's tough to make predictions, especially about the future."

Yogi Berra

Time is an interesting phenomenon. Looking forward, it seems to move slowly, but looking back, it seems to have gone so fast. Strange how that works. We can't adjust it; we can't slow it down nor can we accelerate it. Father Time continues to march onward, at the same pace. For as many things that change over time, how we measure it and the pace has remained untouched.

Analogies and Comparisons

Time and growth go hand in hand, in a sense. A seed needs time to germinate. A cake needs time to bake. Travel takes time, although we have learned to travel at a faster speed. Building muscle takes time. Depending on the item that is being viewed, it could take hours, days, months or even years.

Black walnut trees, native to central and eastern US are grown for their nuts and timber. They can grow three to four inches per year and take roughly 30 years to harvest for timber. You can't plant these trees, water them and check in after three months or even a year with the expectation that you are close to your desired goal. It doesn't work that way. A year into your planting, the tree might stand four feet tall, which is not the optimal time to harvest your crop. Of course, harvesting a sapling sounds ridiculous, but investors often apply this philosophy with their portfolio.

Tend to your retirement dollars as you tend a tree. Manage the expectations over decades, not over news cycles. The success of your forest is dependent upon sun, rain, and time. Investment success (as discussed later in more detail) will be dependent upon contributions, faith, patience, proper diversification, and discipline, among other things.

A healthy body and a healthy financial life have many similarities also. They both require elements of work, attention, and discipline. If today is the first day you decide to eat healthily or hit the gym, you could NOT conclude that you are now healthy. This is merely a step in the right direction of a very long road to health. Even a month of healthy eating or exercising won't solve years of neglect.

Creating long-term wealth sufficient to support a multi-decade retirement is the goal. It is the finish line of all finish lines. Keep this phrase at the forefront: your goal is to create a multi-decade flow of income that your portfolio can support. Although it is the finish line in terms of accumulation, it is the starting line in terms of retirement income. It is the end of your accumulation period and you no longer have that "time" to put money away. Success in retirement, or exercise, is the culmination of the work done over many years to arrive at your goals.

Two Clients Stories

I want to share the story of two clients. They are currently about the same age now, both in their early fifties. Let's call the first one Steve. Steve was one of my first financial planning clients over 20 years ago.

He was making a modest income as an employee, was just starting his family, and had specific goals of accumulating wealth one day. He was determined to set aside 15% of his income towards his long-term accumulation and made that a priority. Every year. And as the years rolled on, Steve became a business owner and although those early years were difficult to save, (he had to invest in his business early on), he kept going and didn't waiver. Now, he contributes the maximum limit allowed in the 401(k), and in some years, he sets aside additional dollars when they are available outside the plan.

Andy came aboard as a client about two years ago and makes about the same amount of money as Steve today. But Andy came to the table with a small IRA along with a 401(k) that he was contributing about 5% of his pay to. He knew retirement was important, but having never worked with an advisor, he just didn't "get around to stepping up his contribution" nor addressing the problem head on. Like many clients I engage with, they are tackling life, taking on the immediate challenges, issues, situations that are presented to them but not looking to the horizon. Retirement is too far off. Hence, they are postponing working on solving this particular issue and thinking they will address it one day down the road.

Keep in mind, that the "day" you retire, you are looking out at the horizon with the longest point of need (in terms of the years you need your money to last). And it is on that day, your spigot of earned income is turned off. So, you need to carefully plan this out: you need to waste as little time (the critical commodity) as you can to accumulate the maximum. Yet, you will waste time. As in most endeavors, waste is common, be it time, money, resources, but that is life. But we must learn from our mistakes and our history.

A Short History Lesson

Let's better understand where retirement was, where it is now and where it is headed. First, keep in mind that retirement is a relatively new phenomenon. For thousands of years, humankind had to work nearly every day to sustain life, albeit shorter than the lives we live today. But let's focus more on modern times and this past century. In 1900, the average person in the United States lived to 47. So, even then, retirement wasn't something that needed some great attention. The population wasn't living long enough to really focus on or worry about "retirement."

But in 1935, right after the Great Depression, President Roosevelt signed into law a social welfare program designed to pay retired workers age 65 or older a continuing income after retirement. Life expectancy in 1930 was about 60 (for males and females), so retirement benefits often didn't get paid. Don't let this point escape you: the government established a safety net for a population that was NOT living to enjoy the fruits of their labor.

What skews these numbers was the high rate of infant mortality at that time, so for those that did attain the age of 65, they could expect to receive benefits for about ten years. Essentially, one worked for 40 years and retirement was a decade, maybe a little more. Take note of this point. Back then, the ratio of working years to retirement years was 4 to 1, maybe even 5 to 1 (in that you could work about 40 years and have just 8 years of a retired life).

Fast forward to today. Life expectancy is almost 80 for a baby born now. The number jumps dramatically for a married couple (that is how long money is needed for the second of the two to pass away) because one is more likely to reach the ripe age of 90. That means, ladies and gentlemen, this married couple will need money to last three decades, maybe even four. For a single person age 65, they will need money to last into their mid-eighties or so.

So, what that means is we are working for 40 years to then support maybe 40 years. That is a 1 to 1 ratio. Waiting until you are in your late forties or early fifties may not give you enough lead in. Consider a larger plane taking off: it needs a longer runway. A retirement plane large enough to sustain a 40-year flight needs a longer runway. You may need all your years of working to save for all of the years of your retirement.

Living to age 100 is a bit more common now, so let's stretch that out. Soon, we will start seeing people living beyond 110. Imagine living more than 40 years in retirement! One will need to plan for that.

For my client Andy, we created a budget and thoroughly examined what was critical and what he could scale down. Then we took the opposite approach to his 401(k), in that we looked at the maximum he could contribute to the plan, which at the time was roughly $24,000 or $2,000 a month. He fully recognized that he had to make a dramatic change here, and though he couldn't make this leap right away, he did ramp up tremendously. When we did some projections, he also saw for the first time that they were going to run out of money in their eighties: that reality hit him hard. There was this "ah ha moment" and he realized that retirement was not going to be exactly what he hoped for, and that working later into his life was less a possibility and more a probability.

Mini Review

Let's review for a brief moment. It used to be you worked four decades to enjoy one in retirement. Today, you still work four decades but you might need monies for three, possibly four decades in retirement. Are you starting to see that those four decades of working are a critical time to save and save as much as you can?

This doesn't even address that for some, we extend our education and training, so whereas most start their working careers at age 21 or 22, there are some who are just starting a graduate program, so their start date is closer to their thirties. Not to mention, many come out with a boat load of debt that then burdens them for decades to come, creating the mindset that loans need greater attention than your future self. Your future self will not send you a "late payment notice" or a "reminder to pay," but you can count on your credit providers to remind you of any late loan payment. Not paying your debts and credit cards will adversely affect your credit; not paying into your retirement account will not. Therefore, it is too easy to say, "I have 30 years until retirement, so I'm not getting into all that just yet." That strain of thinking will get you in trouble. Of course, many will have to battle student loans, credit card debt, hefty mortgage or rent, wedding and divorce expense, education for kids, poor spending habits, and so on and so forth. However, long-term accumulation is at risk. More to the point, YOUR retirement income allotment is what's at stake. YOUR future lifestyle, your freedom, your ability to travel, buy stuff, treat your grandkids and more.

If you use time wisely for those roughly 40 years, then time will be your partner. What you will find is that creating wealth is achievable for anyone who uses time to their advantage. You do not have to be in the top 10% of income earners or even in the top 50%. You just have to look at building wealth as a marathon, not a 100-yard dash. It is slow cooker, not a microwave. Take heed of the gap between what you think will solve the problem and the reality of what actually will solve the problem.

You can retire the word retirement if you think you can only get serious in your fifties. This is where Andy is now, and he understands working is something he will have to do longer than anticipated. Unless you were able to stash away a significant amount, you will lose the most precious element of time, and that has a compounding effect. Exercise your money muscle (of time and compounding) and exorcise your dollar demons of excess spending and being frivolous.

Examples and Numbers

Let's take a look at some compounding examples, where time is your partner.

For this example, let's assume that you contribute $2,000 a year and get a 10% compounded return (no one is promising that) and we look at your account balance at age 66. (This is a hypothetical illustration and does not represent an actual investment. There is no guarantee similar results can be achieved. If fees had been reflected, the return would have been less).

Scenario one

If you are age 26 and contribute your entire working life to age 66, that is 40 years of contributions. 40 multiplied by $2,000 is $80,000 that you invested in total. In this example, we are earning a 10% compound rate of return the entire 40 years (something I would not anticipate, this is just an example). The balance at age 66 is roughly $1,000,000.

Scenario two

Let's back up seven years. At 19, you start to contribute $2,000 per year for only those seven years, until age 26 and earn 10% interest. So, in this scenario, you've contributed just $14,000 cumulative. And then you let that money sit and compound at 10% for the remaining 40 years (not adding any more). At age 66, you have approximately … drum roll please … $1,000,000.

Scenario three

If a newborn child was able to contribute just one payment of $2,000 and then simply let the money compound for 65 years at the same 10% compound return, want to take a guess as to how much that individual would have at age 66? Of course. I don't need to answer.

The point is: the sooner you start, the better off you are. It doesn't matter what you did PRIOR to reading this, from this point on, you now know what needs to be done. And if you choose NOT to act, then your lack of accumulation is on you. Whatever time you have left until retirement, you need to take advantage of it. Not easy to do, but rather simple to grasp. You just can't afford to waste any more time.

We've established that the compounding effect enhances accumulating monies when you have long periods. Now let's look at one more compounding example to get a better grasp on how it works. If you save a penny and double the savings every day for a single month (31 days), how much will you have at day 31? Starting with the first week, .01, then .02, then .04, .08, .16, .32 and .64, so after one week, you have 64 cents.

Want to take any guess where you are at the end of day 31? Stop reading and give this a moment's thought. This is not a math question you can figure out but just take a guess. Put the book down just for one moment and think about your guess.

Welcome back …

Okay, week 2, let's continue: 1.28, 2.56, 5.12, 10.24, 20.48, 40.96 and 81.92. End of week 2, you are at roughly $82.

Week 3 (at this point, I'll remove the cents): 163, 327, 655, 1310, 2,621, 5,242 and 10,485.

Did we blow past your original guess? Pause here for another moment, do you want to revise your original guess?

Week 4: 20,971, 41,943, 83,886, 167,772, 335,544, 671,088 and 1,342,177. After 28 days, we topped $1,000,000.

But still not done. A few more days.

Day 29 is 2,684,354.

Day 30 is 5,368,708.

Day 31 is 10,737,417.

That is correct my dear readers, almost $11 million.

Now, of course, you are **not** going to double your money when you invest it but let's extract something interesting here. Say you have 31 YEARS till retirement and you double your money annually. (I want you to understand how compounding works, so forget for the moment that doubling your money won't happen, but this will highlight the point I want to get across about compounding.) Suppose you said, "I have 31 years to retirement, I'm going to wait 1 year to get started," in this scenario, what does that one-year cost?

The increase from year 30 to year 31, (the $5,300,000 to $10,700,000 does NOT happen). By delaying just one single year, the cost of that delay is $5,300,000 of the $10,700,000. You see, you will always cross the threshold of a penny going to two cents, but you do NOT cross the threshold on the back end. The cost of waiting means it's the back end that you miss out on. But we don't see that when we make the decision on the front end.

One more time. If you decide to wait two years to get started, then you don't see the growth from the $2,500,000 on (from year 29 to year 31), so the cost is over $7,500,000 of the nearly $11,000,000. The cost is the majority of the account. Can you now see how powerful compounding is? We really need the time; we need that supercharge to take place to get us the accumulation that we require.

Of course, I want all clients to be more like Steve than Andy, but I don't get to choose that, nor do clients have that option in the context of where they are in that moment. Meaning, the problem of inadequate retirement accumulation is rampant, and logically knowing about the problem in your twenties or thirties isn't enough to motivate consumers to readily address it. We, as financial advisors can only help clients when they are ready to be helped, so sometimes, that is early and sometimes that is late … sometimes too late to accumulate enough to fully support the retirement the client desired. Regardless, you need to get started and get something stockpiled for later, even if it runs short of your desired amount.

In Other Aspects of Our Life

This behavior is common in society today. We see it in our health. See a doctor regularly, maybe you can catch things early. But the doctor can't prevent all health issues, so you can still get sick. But ignore the problem, allow symptoms to grow and not get medical attention, sometimes the physician can't resolve the health issue because you addressed it too late.

Maybe you can't fully resolve your retirement problem, but if you have children starting out at work, then I would highly encourage you to pass these lessons on to them. Don't let them make the mistake you made. This may be difficult, trying to get your children to listen to you (as my wife always said, "You can't be a prophet in your own land"), but passing on the book can do the trick.

You need to get started yesterday, but since we can't go back, you need to get started immediately. Do not waste any more of the precious commodity of time. Your Black Walnut forest can't wait any longer for you to plant the seeds. We need time to be our friend, not our enemy.

Action Items:

- You must first understand your time horizon. What is your estimate of years you have to work before retirement?

- You would then be wise to understand from a compounding point of view, what could you save/invest and at some reasonable growth rate and calculate what that will grow to. With that figure, ask yourself, is that a figure I could reasonably retire on?

- If the answer is no or not even close, you will need to take a hard look at extending the time horizon and/or finding ways to reduce current spending so you can increase annual contributions. Remember, this is your life, your lifestyle in those later years, so addressing this is all about you.

CHAPTER 5

Insurance

"Those who have knowledge don't predict. Those who predict don't have knowledge."

Lao Tzu

No financial guide would be complete if it didn't address certain lines of insurance. There are many traditional lines of insurance, as well as some lesser used solutions. In this chapter, we are only going to address a few of them: life insurance, disability, and long-term care.

The section about life insurance is dedicated to the personal use of planning, not a business use. There are a multitude of needs that require life insurance on business owners but that is not our focus here.

The premise for buying insurance, any insurance, is to pass risk. If you do not want to pass it on, then you bear it. The cost to pass it on is called the premium. By not passing it, doesn't mean you are able to "dodge it" or eliminate that said risk. You only save the premium at the risk of the event occurring. So, if you don't pass it, then the potential cost is now the event happening, and it's only logical to ascertain that the cost of the event happening could be tremendous, sometimes immeasurable in terms of dollars.

More often, consumers think about the odds of the event occurring, and if those odds are low, they sometimes choose not to pass that risk. The element that most people don't readily think of is NOT what the odds are but what is the CONSEQUENCE of the event occurring. What would become of your family if a death occurred or a disability or the need for medical care? This is the question that needs addressing. The odds are more relevant to the insurance company in how they may price the product, but the consequence comes into play with regards to protecting your family.

An important and differentiating element (compared to other products you buy) about insurance is insurability. This is a critical point in that insurance is unlike most any other product you acquire. You do NOT buy insurance; you APPLY for it. Meaning, you could get turned down. Or, you could be rated. Rated means that you will be paying more for the coverage. For example, if your health is not very good, then insurance companies have the right to charge you a higher premium because you are a higher risk to them. Insurance companies are being asked to bear risk and the likelihood of death for a smoker is greater than that of someone that doesn't smoke and is in excellent health, so premiums on these two people would not be the same (if they were the same age).

You will want to buy insurance BEFORE you need it. You can't call your property insurance agent up while your house is burning down and request fire insurance. If you have a serious medical issue, then it might be too late to buy life insurance. At some point, many of us cross over from insurable to uninsurable. Do not take this element lightly. Insurance can be postponed to the point when you exclude yourself from ever being able to get it. Discuss this in greater detail with your advisor or insurance agent.

Life Insurance

Life insurance is one of those staple purchases for most. Like many financial strategies, there is no "one right way" to address this but there are many wrong ways. With that, let's look at a few questions we want to address:

When should one buy life insurance? Typically, you should buy life insurance when someone is dependent upon you in some capacity. If your death results in a financial loss, then life insurance should be considered. For example, a married couple with a child (or children), with one spouse working and one raising the kids, the obvious choice would be to buy insurance for the working spouse because there is a direct loss of money. Depending on your situation, that stay-at-home spouse should consider having protection. We are not comparing what each brings to the household from a financial standpoint; we are addressing what the loss would be.

The employed spouse is obvious in terms of seeing the need for insurance but the loss of the non-employed spouse creates a hole in the family, too. A family with young kids will need someone to look after them (cost of day care), transporting them to and from schools, doctors, programs, activities and more. But something else to think about: let's say the working spouse earns enough to fully cover these costs and expenses. The question now becomes, does that person WANT to be the sole breadwinner while someone else has to "raise" the kids or does that person now want an option to cut back on their working life to be there more for the kids. Having the insurance on the non-employed spouse gives that breadwinner an option. Meaning, instead of the employed spouse putting in long hours for a large income, maybe they can cut back. Maybe they spend more time at home or taking the kids to school or picking them up, which means less hours working. Which correlates to making less. So, THAT is where we need insurance dollars to make up for that lost income. This spouse is now choosing to forgo earned income (while the kids are young) and making it up by having a life-insurance policy on the non-employed spouse to give them some "breathing room" if they want to step back for a period of years. Not all professions might allow this, but if yours does, then insurance on the non-employed spouse is just as important as the employed spouse.

Now comes the question of how much? This can get complicated, so let me offer up three ways to determine an amount.

Random amount. This is the most commonly used method today. Years ago, when the life insurance industry was greater represented in terms of a career choice, other methods were taught, promoted, and followed. But career life-insurance agents have gone the way of door-to-door encyclopedia salespeople (a slight exaggeration but you get the picture). So, this random round-number method is arbitrary. $1,000,000 is common. As if to say, $1,000,000 will solve everyone's insurance needs. This is an acceptable method, but it does require more thought than to just stamp the same solution onto every scenario. Don't fall into the trap of buying insurance on the amount of the mortgage balance. That is a common solution and is woefully short. Make sure some thought is given to the situation by taking debt, education, kids, and years of income into account. If you want to be more specific, then the following method will calculate these amounts to produce a number, whereas the random method estimates.

Needs analysis. This was the most common method the traditional life-insurance salesperson was taught years ago. But again, the industry of this being a career occupation has diminished over the past few decades, so the method of solving needs has changed. Needs analysis is about determining your gross needs and subtracting your current resources. For example, there are typically two elements to evaluating your needs, your debts and then your ongoing income needs. The debts are rather easy to calculate: just add up the cost of the mortgage, student loans, credit card debt, car loans and such. Keep in mind kids' future education, such as the private school, college, and graduate programs that you might want to have money set aside for.

Then, you need to determine future income and how many additional dollars you may need over however many years. This gets a bit more complicated because one needs to take into account a growth rate, as well as estimate the unknown of those future years. Once you have the "number" for both of those pieces, then you subtract out the resources you have (savings, retirement accounts, investment portfolios and more).

For example, let's say you have a $350,000 mortgage, $35,000 car loan, $15,000 home equity, two kids aged seven and five, have $20,000 in savings and $500,000 in a retirement account. And let's assume your kids will attend public school, but you would like to cover their college costs (your parents left you with college loans that took you 15 years to knock out and you don't wish to do the same for your kids). To cover the current debt, not including education, we need $400,000. Keep in mind, this does not give any extra for unknowns or a cushion.

College could cost over $100,000 a year for a private school by the time these kids go, and a public school could cost roughly half, so setting aside the higher amount, we might need $500,000 for EACH kid. That is $1,500,000 not including income element. We might also need 20 years of income (growing with the rising cost of goods). Our expenses are lower as we might not have a mortgage or might not have education costs (these are addressed in the number above), but we do have living expenses, so if we need $50,000 a year for 20 years, then that will be roughly another $1,000,000 (not taking into account the time value of money). So, our total need is approximately $2,500,000. Needs analysis would then subtract out the $500,000 that you have in the retirement account, so the net need would be $2,000,000. In this example, I would consider buying the $2,500,000 or even $3,000,000 life insurance policy to give a little buffer (for the many unknowns out there).

Keep in mind, when we address the type of insurance to purchase, one solution is term insurance[1] and that initial cost is very reasonable, so

---

1 Premiums will increase at the time the policy is renewed. All guarantees are based on the financial strength and claims paying ability of the issuing insurance company, who is solely responsible for all obligations under its policies. Products and services may not be available in all states. The amount of benefits provided depends upon the plan selected and that the premium will vary with the amount of the benefits selected. Riders and conversion provisions are subject to additional costs.

that additional $500,000 in premium cost is manageable in the budget. If you didn't pass that risk, then you are bearing it. If the event occurs (death happens), then the cost (exposure) is over $2,000,000. That is a steep figure. Premiums won't be nearly that figure (obviously).

Human life value. The last of the methods was crafted by Solomon Huebner in the early 1900s. He was responsible for the Chartered Life Underwriter's Designation awarded by the American College, which involved passing ten courses of higher education specific to the life-insurance industry using the Human Life Value (HLV) theory. The concept deals with human capital, which is a person's income potential. Oversimplifying here, essentially each life has a value based on the future earnings of that person's occupation and age. For example, it might be 20 times your income at younger ages and then 18 times as you get older to 15 times and so forth.

The difference with HLV compared to needs analysis is that you don't subtract what you currently have in resources. Essentially, you can look at HLV as the "gross" need and needs analysis is a net need.

When the 9/11 terrorist attacks occurred, the government decided to pay the heirs of those who perished in the attacks via a modified formula of HLV. What they did differently was subtracting the individual insurance that some of the people owned. For example, if your HLV was $1,500,000 and you owned a $1,000,000 policy, they then covered you for $500,000.

Underwriters of insurance companies typically look at HLV as the top end with regards to how much coverage one can buy. Contrary to what a consumer might think, you cannot buy as much insurance as you want. Some people think they are over-insured, but insurance companies and underwriters would not typically allow that to happen. They have upper limits on how much a person can own. Just because you can afford $5,000,000 of term insurance doesn't mean a company will issue it. If you can afford to buy 100,000 pens from your office supply store, they will sell them to you, regardless of your needs or ability to use them over your life. Not the case with life insurance: you cannot be over insured.

Oftentimes, consumers look at premiums and see it as a lot of money. If the premium is expensive in their eyes, then what is the benefit? But NOT getting the benefit if the event occurs is what is expensive. Imagine this family above NOT having insurance and a death occurs … then what? They're in trouble, that's what.

What Type of Insurance?

This is where things can really get complicated, so for the purposes of this book, I am going to keep this at a broad level analysis. There are more detailed sources and it is certainly worth working with an advisor, but for now let's explore the landscape.

Term Insurance

This is the least expensive form of insurance, initially. I want to highlight the word, initially. You are essentially paying for mortality costs. It used to be that term premiums would rise annually, but the industry now has fixed rates for 10, 20 and even 30 years. So, one can buy a tremendous amount of protection and keep the rates level for two or three decades. After the level rate, the premium jumps so high that most likely you will not keep the coverage. So, plan on keeping it for that fixed-rate period; you can always cancel it prior to the level period ending. The rate cannot be increased by the insurance company during that term, even if your health declines in that period (as long as you pay the premium).

A client of mine, let's call him Mike, purchased a $1,000,000 20-year term policy in 1999 when he was in great health. He was 33, married, and a father of two young kids. Fast forward, I recently received a letter from the insurance company that stated, come the end of 2019 (the end of his 20 years of level rates), the premium was going to increase from $132 a month to $1,632 a month for the next year and rise annually thereafter. There is context in this relationship that might help. Our relationship went separate ways, but the client kept the policy. I reached out to him to make sure he knew his premium was going to dramatically change. In the conversation, he shared with me, that he'd had a pacemaker put in. Had you looked at this guy, you would have seen a picture of health. He ate healthily and exercised often but had a heart issue. He had crossed over from being insurable (at the time of purchase) to being uninsurable now. Certainly, his needs were different. His kids were now grown and out of the house, but do you think Mike would like to keep his coverage for 10 or 20 years longer? Do you think he's okay with the cost of coverage skyrocketing so much that keeping it made no sense?

In this situation, the term policy had a conversion right where the client can convert the term to permanent, so he will be able to keep the coverage for the rest of his life. The premium will be higher than the term cost for those 20 years but it will be manageable, but most important, the coverage will continue when his insurability dictates he wouldn't be able to get other coverage.

If you have young kids, I strongly suggest using a combination of a 20- and 30-year level term. This gets the kids "out of the house" and keeps coverage a little longer. But just because the kids are out does not mean the need (or want) for protection ends. The reality of life is that some kids might stay "on the payroll" longer than expected and our retirement nest egg won't be as large as we need, so additional years of protection may be needed.

The strength and value of term insurance is you can get a tremendous amount for a fixed period at a reasonable cost, but the downside is you do not "own" it. You are renting it for that period. My client, Mike, knew this when he purchased that insurance in 1999, and the insurance served his needs over that time frame. Certainly, things changed at the tail end of his 20-year period, but all in all, the product served its purpose.

Statistically speaking, you will pay for coverage that you won't access as most people who buy term insurance live beyond the term limits. But that is a good thing. Term insurance also offers a conversion feature (as described in what Mike did above), meaning it allows the insured to change it to another form of insurance and you then pay a new premium for the product going forward. So, you can convert from term to permanent if you felt the need or desire to keep the coverage longer.

Permanent Insurance

This is tremendously complicated, so this is where we will take that view from 50,000 feet. There are three types.

Whole life. This is the oldest form, dating back more than 150 years. Whole life is priced to age 100 (but there are variations), and the insured pays a lifetime level premium and the benefit is in force to the day you die (could be after age 100). The insurance company collects a greater amount in the early years to support that larger costs in those later years (mortality costs rise every year, because every year you get older, you stand a greater chance of dying). For paying that extra premium early, they offer an incentive of building cash value or equity in the policy. These dollars are based on their general portfolio of the company, which is usually a conservative, mostly bond-driven asset. So, cash value products tend to be in line with that conservative bond portfolio. There are tax incentives for whole life policies, like no taxation on the cash value growth year to year, meaning there are no 1099s at tax time. The longer one lives, the better these policies work. Term is the opposite. The longer you live with term, you could outlive your coverage years (like Mike did) and the policy collapses. Whole life pays dividends, and over time these dollars grow to the point where they can cover the premiums, so there are instances where essentially the policy can support itself and no more premiums are required to be paid by the insured. This is a strong long-term benefit of whole life.

One of my clients purchased a large whole life policy for his son, Eric, at the age of 20 (this was the end of 1993), to jumpstart his son's insurance portfolio. About seven years later, Eric joined us at a review meeting to discuss the policy. At the time, he recently invested monies in the stock market and was experiencing tremendous growth. He commented that had he taken those premium dollars, he would have been far more ahead in terms of growth than the cash value of the insurance policy. Yes, he was correct, but whole life insurance was never meant to compete with investing monies, so this was an unfair comparison. Eric nearly decided to cancel the policy but ended up keeping it. The next few years (2000–2002), the stock market dropped, and Eric, lost a significant portion of his portfolio (upwards of 90% on some of the stocks). Fast forward, and we are now 20-plus years into his insurance and the cash value is six digits. Every year, he gets his premium and calls me and tells me it's his favorite bill of the year. Because he knows the cash value will grow greater than his annual premiums. It just gets better every year. And on top of the cash value growth, his insurance protection is also growing. He has nearly twice the original death benefit that he owns, meaning there is no time limit like term insurance. I love taking that call annually. This is not about comparing which solution is better at all: both (permanent insurance and investing monies) have merits and must be examined individually for where they fit and what makes most sense.

Universal Life Insurance

This blossomed in the mid-80s when interest rates spiked. The product offers cash value growth based on current interest rates, so back then it was very attractive. But, at the time, it didn't offer a guaranteed premium, guaranteed death benefit, or guaranteed cash value like whole life insurance did. And eventually, when interest rates dropped, these products imploded. But the insurance industry modified the product and came up with a guaranteed death benefit solution, and if you pay the minimum amount to support the death benefit, you can design a solution today that is essentially term insurance for a longer period than 30 years. You can run it out to age 100 or longer, and the premiums will be larger than term but could be lower than whole life. You can select premium levels to just cover the death benefit or you can choose higher premiums to accumulate some cash value. This is a wonderful solution for longer term death benefit needs if you don't want to pay higher premiums for whole life. There are several variations of universal life, so working with an insurance professional who can compare and contrast the many versions will help.

Variable Life Insurance[2]

This product took flight after interest rates fell and the stock market started to take off in the 1990s, so this product is tied more to current equity investments. Whereas whole life is tied to a portfolio of the insurance company and is mostly bonds, here the consumer can decide what to invest in and they take on that risk.

Today, the insurance industry has combined these variations into quite complex products to solve the needs of consumer, so evaluating various forms will serve you best. Don't just look at the cheapest rate as the only criteria. Cost might be the overriding factor, but consider longevity and how to solve the bigger picture of needs.

---

2 Variable life insurance products, which are subject to market risk including possible loss of principal, allow the contract holder to choose an appropriate amount of life insurance protection that has an additional cost associated with it. Care should be taken to ensure these strategies and products are suitable for your long-term life insurance needs. You should weigh your objectives, time horizon and risk tolerance as well as any associated costs before investing. Also, be aware that market volatility can lead to the possibility of the need for additional premium in your policy. Variable life insurance has fees and charges associated with it that include costs of insurance that vary with such characteristics of the insured as gender, health and age, underlying fund charges and expenses, and additional charges for riders that customize a policy to fit your individual needs. The sub-accounts in variable insurance products fluctuate with market conditions and when surrendered the principal may be worth more or less than the original amount invested. All guarantees are subject to the claims-paying ability of the issuing insurance company. Guarantees do not apply to the investment performance of any variable accounts, which are subject to market risk.

The various permanent products have morphed over the years and they have a layer of complexity. The important element here is they each offer something; they extend the longevity of owning the insurance and, in turn, give insureds greater peace of mind. There is no "right" solution; each presents something of value.

One of the key elements when looking at variations of universal, variable or combinations is evaluating if and when the policy might implode. Paying a minimal premium puts you at risk of the policy running out and, most likely, you will not want this to happen, so discuss this with your advisor and look over the figures at not only the time of purchase but every two or three years to make sure it is on track.

Keep in mind, entire books are dedicated to these solutions, so trying to fit this into one chapter does not do the product full justice, but the goal here is to start the conversation and for you to continue it with an advisor to better guide you along the way.

Where Do You Buy Insurance?

Many lines of insurances are complicated, so my strong suggestion is to find a trusted relationship that you can work with. Certainly, buying direct from companies avoids "pesky salespeople" (they are often seen in this negative light when in fact, most are good people looking out for their clients' needs), but professionals in the industry often offer value. Although term insurance is pretty straightforward, the other lines are quite complicated, so it's better to have someone review the options at the time of purchase and service and support the product on an ongoing basis. A fiduciary advisor is bound to a professional code that means they are looking out for your best interests. If you don't work with a fiduciary, your option may be working with a salesperson, and they are not held to that same standard. They might be representing a company or product, so you will want to ask the person you are working if they are a fiduciary. That is the highest standard.

When it comes to companies, a good default option is to select one with a higher rating. All companies are measured by various rating agencies, so explore those metrics. Not all companies offer all the products discussed, so seek out companies that not only have those lines but are leaders in those specific products. Oftentimes, a professional can assist in this arena. Many companies do not offer traditional whole life policies or disability or long-term care products, so you will have to seek which ones do.

Disability Insurance

Disability insurance seems to have always been the most avoided mainstream protection product, yet it is arguably one of the most important. The following statements are designed for the masses, and keep in mind that there are exceptions to these broad positions.

Your income dictates your lifestyle. It is your income that supports your needs, desires, and wants. It is also your income that pays for the various other insurances (life, homeowners, auto, health). But what protects the income? What if your income stopped, could you generate income? This is the analogy of the goose and the golden egg, where we focus on protecting the "egg" but ignore insuring the goose. Auto and homeowner's insurance protect "things," but what bought those things was your income, so what is protecting the goose that generates that golden egg of income? Oftentimes, nothing.

We don't readily see ourselves getting disabled. We see ourselves dying (not yet or soon) because we know that will happen one day. But being disabled? We don't really see that, so we often choose not to protect against that risk. It is an avoidable insurance, and most do avoid it, unlike auto insurance or homeowner's insurance, which are mandatory. You can avoid the act of buying disability insurance but of course, you can't avoid the reality of something bad happening in life that results in your inability to work.

The premise behind disability insurance is it protects you if are unable to work. The definitions vary here, but for simplicity's sake, if one is sick or injured, then that is the starting point. Keep in mind that the insurance we are referring to, individual long-term disability, protects against a claim that might be years long or permanent and benefits often run to age 65. (There are other products out there that cover short-term disability benefits, but we are not evaluating those solutions.)

Think about this, if you save 10% of your income, with no growth, then it takes ten years to save one year of income. If you were unable to work for a period of time, how long would it take (if you became disabled) until you cleared out your savings? Remember what we discussed earlier about not making a decision based on the odds but about examining the consequences. Not being able to work can be devastating for most, especially given that many of us are only a few months away from serious trouble in terms of not having accumulated sufficient savings.

Disability insurance protects this risk exposure. And most contracts offer benefits to age 65. Consider two job offers, which one would you take?

Job A – Salary $100,000. If you become disabled, you get zero income or benefits.

Job B – Salary $97,500. If you become disabled, you get $5,000 a month (tax free) to age 65.

In short, disability insurance protects your greatest asset: your income. Your income is what supports you, buys your things, pays for the mortgage, pays for your lifestyle. Why wouldn't you want to protect that? Consider roughly 3% of your income to protect your income (meaning, it costs roughly 3% of your income that could be your premium but the premium is dependent on your age, occupational risk, contract language and riders).

Do not ignore this line of insurance. The consequence could be devastating. If you really want to get an interesting viewpoint, find someone who is or was disabled and ask them what they think of the product. Ask them if they had it or wish they had it. Of course, you can ask someone who has never been disabled, but to get the full view, find someone who was out of work for a year or more and I suspect their conviction will be deep.

My Client Jeffrey

In my second year in the business, I took on a new client, Jeffrey, and after evaluations and comparisons, he purchased a large whole-life policy (with a rider called "waiver of premium") and a disability policy. Jeff owned a printing press that he started when he was a kid and it grew to a nice business over the years. The image that is probably coming to your mind was the same as mine when we discussed disability: his arm or hand getting caught in a machine. About three years into our relationship, Jeffrey experienced various health issues and his body developed an allergic reaction to the chemicals in the press room. Since the chemicals were everywhere in the workplace, his doctor ordered him out of the building. This led to filing a disability claim that was awarded along with the insurance company paying his whole-life policy (because he had the waiver of premium rider). The printing business was all Jeffrey knew, so these disability income payments that were coming in monthly sustained his living. I can't imagine where he would be without those monthly checks coming in. Three decades later, Jeffrey is still receiving benefits. He purchased a lifetime benefit on the disability policy, so the insurance company will be paying him for his life. His son is Eric, mentioned earlier. Jeffrey believed so greatly in the products that he started his son early on that whole-life policy. A gift of tremendous value.

Long-Term Care Insurance [3]

Long-term care insurance (LTC) is a relatively new product offered by insurance companies. And they are still trying to properly price it. The triggers for LTC are different than disability insurance, but the idea has similar roots in that monies are supporting a form of lifestyle. LTC pays when two of the six activities of daily living (ADLs) can't be performed by the person or cognitive impairment: eating, bathing, dressing, continence, toileting and transferring. The landscape is dramatically changing for LTC products; new solutions are cropping up and insurance companies are being creative in product design.

LTC is more often purchased when people get closer to retirement. If you purchase it at a younger age, you can lock in premiums with certain types of contracts. Policies have morphed over the years, and they typically fall into several categories:

- Traditional
- Asset based
- Life insurance with LTC rider

Traditional LTC insurance provides protection if the need of LTC arises. There is a possibility that you could not use the benefits of a traditional product. Like several other lines of insurance (e.g.

---

3 Policy benefits may be reduced by any policy loans, withdrawals, terminal illness benefit, or long-term care benefits paid under the policy. Death Proceeds and Return of Premium Benefit will be reduced when long-term care benefits are taken. Values assume no prior distributions of any kind taken. Certain benefits may not be available until a specific age is attained. An elimination period may apply before long-term care benefits are available. See your policy for details. The monthly amount reimbursed is the cost of covered long-term care expenses actually incurred, which may be less than the Monthly Maximum Benefit. The Monthly Maximum Benefit may be pro-rated based on the actual number of days that the insured is chronically ill or confined to a facility. Long-term care insurance benefits may be subject to limitations, waiting periods, and other restrictions.

homeowners), if you never file a claim, you won't reap the benefits other than to give you "peace of mind." There are no residual values or death benefits in these contracts. This is a "use it or lose it" solution.

The other forms of LTC insurance (**asset-based contracts and life insurance with an LTC rider**), more broadly speaking, offer variations of possible cash growth and/or death benefit. So, if you never have a need for the LTC portion, upon your demise there will be a benefit paid to your heirs, so all is not lost. Like life insurance, these products can get complicated, so having a trusted relationship is key to the overall selection and implementation.

I want to keep the conversation of LTC insurance to a very broad level, not because the product demands little attention, but because it's more important to evaluate your options with your advisor to find a solution that best suits you. As noted, there are no universal "right answers" on any of these insurances, and the help of a trusted advisor will pay dividends.

The cost of care today is usually measured in a daily dollar amount and can be in the $200 to $300 per day range. If you find that passing the risk to that extent is too great a cost, then strongly consider getting some coverage while bearing some of the exposure. Having a $200 per day benefit will ease the financial burden if you need care. Claims statistically tend to average roughly two to three years, so a four- to six-year benefit period will give sound coverage, but keep in mind that Alzheimer's and dementia care could require benefits to be paid out for considerably longer.

One last point on buying LTC insurance: you may want to consider an inflation rider if you're young so the cost of the benefit rises over the years. If you buy the policy at 58 and don't claim until 74, then the monthly benefit will have grown all those years.

In summary, the question that often seems to be the starting point is "How much does insurance cost?" That is a legitimate and reasonable question when exploring where it fits. But it cannot be the sole driver or determinant. You must also ask, "What is the cost of NOT insuring and having the death/disability/need for support happen?"

Consider both sides of the equation. Premiums are NEVER the problem; they are the solution to the potential problem. Of course, we don't like paying premiums, but even worse is having bad "stuff" happen to us and having to pay out of pocket. Insurance is a critical component to building a sound, well-balanced financial plan. And it is a solution that often requires working with a trusted advisor, one that knows you, understands your situation and can offer solutions that best serve you. Take some time to vet and interview those who represent insurance products. Ask questions about their background of insurance, their philosophy, how they represent it, who they represent and more. You want an advisor or broker who has the ability to work with many companies. Some insurance agents are tied to companies and cannot represent other solutions in the marketplace, so you will want to be aware of that. Ask lots of questions, don't be shy here.

Action Items:

- Take an inventory of your overall insurance and discuss with an independent advisor to see where, if at all, there are gaps and shortages.

- For life insurance, think through what if a death occurs: consider who would be financially affected and to what extent they could support themselves. Then explore what that cost would be to close those gaps. Compare that premium cost to their shortage.

- Before rejecting the idea of both disability insurance and LTC, seek to find someone or several who have experienced the need for this coverage and see what they have to say. Most likely, you will get the painful truth about mistakes they made and what they would have done differently.

CHAPTER 6

Savings

"It matters not how far the journey, so long as you don't stop."

Confucius

Savings accounts are often the overlooked piece of the financial puzzle, but in this chapter, we are going to take a long hard look at what you need to do to help promote your success. Let's make a distinction between a passbook savings account and a checking account or even a debit card account. The idea of a savings account is to have a holding account, whereas checking and debit accounts are more for the transfer of monies (to pay bills and buy stuff).

Money can be broken into three broad categories of use: save, spend, and invest. Savings is the least attractive, spending oftentimes gives us joy and investing allows us to see a future with money. Savings then, tends to be a category we often ignore.

Let's look at savings in two broad phases:

1. Long before retirement (accumulation years of our life)
2. Close to retirement (about ten years before our desired retirement age)

How to Save Long Before Retirement

One will need to have the security that savings presents, so work towards not minimizing the importance of saving, in spite of the appearance that it doesn't benefit you. That security is huge. The second critical element of savings is segregating your monies. Simply stated, you will need to save money, and when you do, allot monies for specific purposes and do not commingle these various needs.

For example, here are a few of the accounts I would strongly suggest opening (but not limited to these):

Pure savings. In this account, I suggest you stash away three to six months' worth of monthly expenses. If you own a business, then three months is acceptable (if not, six). If your monthly expenses are $5,000, this account should therefore be roughly $15,000. If you want to squeeze a little "juice" here, you can use varying-length CDs[4] to generate a little more return than a passbook savings account. So, maybe $5,000 is in a two-year CD, $5,000 is in an 18-month CD, and $5,000 in a regular savings (or something like that). The optimal goal here is that these dollars just "sit there" and provide security. They are your security blanket when things go awry. And if you ever have to dip into these dollars, find a way to replenish them when time and money allow. Do not take the posture that your money is being wasted or just sitting idle. Although it is, it is giving you that security. Comfort is a valuable, healthy emotion.

Put in and take out. This account is what most people refer to as savings. Problem is, there is little security here because most are putting in and taking out. As you take dollars out, I would then suggest you replenish the account over time. This account can have a specific dollar balance, like $5,000. Once you reach that number, no more deposits.

---

4 Bank certificates of deposit are FDIC insured up to applicable limits and offer a fixed rate of return. [Variable annuity returns/mutual fund yields] and principal will fluctuate with market conditions.

This is the account that you go to if you need say, new tires. Go ahead and charge the tires but do NOT keep any balance on a charge card from month to month. Use this account to help pay off that balance for a purchase larger than your monthly ability to reasonably pay the bill.

House / vacation. This account is to be used for the larger purchases for the house or the top-dollar vacation. So, for example, if you needed an end table for your den (and it's not a lot of money), go ahead and purchase it and pay for it out of your regular bills. But if you need a new dining room set or need to add on a back yard deck, i.e. a big-ticket item, it's best to save up for it and take the dollars from this account when you can. An item like a European trip or a major renovation takes months to plan and research, so use that time to "sock money away." These dollars are not investable dollars. Investment dollars have short-term risk, meaning markets can drop and if so, we don't want to expose these dollars to market gyrations. For my house account, I've taken it one step further and created a spreadsheet of various projects that require funding over time. That spreadsheet shows the current dollars allocated to that particular project. The actual savings account is one figure, but the spreadsheet breaks it down multiple ways. At any given time, I will have several projects and goals that I am saving for and this segregation gives me the freedom to focus and spend while not adversely affecting something else.

Kids/education. The idea of investing monies for education is largely taken up using a 529 College Savings Plan.[5] Each state has options

---

5 There is no guarantee that the plan will grow to cover college expenses. In addition, 529 college savings plans may be available only if you invest in the home state's 529 college savings plan. Any state-based benefit offered with respect to a particular 529 college savings plan should be one of many appropriately weighted factors to be considered in making an investment decision. You should consult with your financial, tax or other advisor to learn more about how state-based benefits (including any limitations) would apply to your specific circumstances and also may wish to contact your home state or any other 529 college savings plan to learn more about the features, benefits and limitations of that state's 529 college savings plan. You may also go to www.collegesavings.org for more information.

for consumers to invest in mutual funds and get certain tax advantages if used for higher education. Recently, tax law changes have allowed these accounts to be used for a limited amount of other schooling. But this section is not about the use or value of a 529 plan (they are of tremendous value); this is about establishing a liquidity account for various costs that come along with having a child or children. With that, you will need monies prior to college for a whole host of items. So, have a cushion for these upcoming expenses, such as help buying a car or special celebrations, like a graduation party or even a larger graduation gift. And when the kids are then done with education, you can change that account title to a "wedding" account. Keeping it with the kids' theme, weddings today are a bloody fortune, and it is expected that both families will pay for wedding expenses.

Segregating your accounts gives you freedom. Freedom to spend the money in that particular account. If you saved for a vacation or to re-do a room in the house, then funds that are allotted to that project don't affect other things. Of course, you need to build the pure savings and put-and-take account as your initial accounts, but along the way, you can also build the house/vacation account simultaneously.

Savings is about liquidity. It really has little to do with growth given historic low interest rates and more to do with having a safety net. But make no mistake here: these accounts are critical to success. This is a team game, and every aspect of the financial equation warrants attention. This may not be the most exciting piece, but it is a foundation item that offers support.

Creative Thoughts to Spur on Savings

Let's get a little creative in thinking about how we can save a few extra dollars along the way. Just like you will budget your investing dollars, you will need to budget savings dollars. Allot a certain amount each month to fund at least one if not more of these savings accounts. Discipline is required. You must also budget for what you give yourself as cash.

On the subject of budgeting cash, here is another thought on how to save in a unique way. Let's say you budget $200 every two weeks for cash expenses. At the end of a two week stretch, you have $40 left in your wallet. The question now becomes, do you take $160 for that next two-week timeframe or do you still take the $200 that you budgeted? Let's say you take the $200 that you budgeted, the next question is what do you do with the $40 that was left over? I know, you have probably never give this situation or scenario any thought. Well, I want you to now because if you play these cards right, you will have a little reward down the road. But, like so many other aspects of your financial life, you will need to develop the habit of discipline. Not an easy trait to develop but the results are rewarding.

Here is my suggestion. Take that $40 and stick in in an envelope. When that envelope reaches $100, take it to the bank and get a $100 bill. And every time you don't spend your allotted budget, set it aside and collect $100 bills. Why? The funny thing about a $100 bill is how we value it. For example, let's say you have two envelopes, and both with $100 in them. One has five $20 bills and one has a $100 bill. If you think about ordering a pizza to be delivered and are short on funds in your wallet, are you more tempted to order that pizza if you have the envelope of twenties? Most of us don't like to break a large dollar bill. Use basic psychology to save!

In poker games, there is an expression that if you don't go into a hand and lose money, then those chips you might have lost are now earned by you. Along those same lines, if you don't spend money, the dollars not spent are considered saved. Make a few more "smarter" decisions during the year, and when you look back, you will see those results, maybe in the form of a few Franklins sitting in an envelope.

Let me share another silly game to play, that will no doubt yield results. Start with a $5 bill and a cup (or again, an envelope). Every time you get a $5 bill, add it to the cup. You won't notice the $5 missing in your wallet. If you add your $5 bills you have accumulated up in a month, you won't be excited. But do this for six months or a year and you'll find a bonus present under the tree. It's almost like found money. I started this and decided not to spend it, and after a couple years I found I accumulated a few thousand dollars. Then I "graduated" to $10 bills to see if I could double the fun. Try it. My cups and envelopes, over time started to become meaningful numbers. And they were separate from my savings accounts, my checking account, my investment accounts. These were pockets of "found monies" for me. Eventually, the discipline to play these games over time becomes habit forming.

I have taken these strategies to the next level, and I continue to use some of them. Pick one or two and see what you can do over a year's timeframe. And if you are successful in saving something that you would not have saved before, then step up your game the next year. This is creating your own security.

Savings Just Prior to Retirement

Let's now address the savings plan you will want at (and before) retirement. But to accomplish this goal, we will need to start looking at this about ten years before, maybe 15, but a decade of planning can accomplish what we need to do. At this point in your life, most likely, the kids' accounts and education are behind you (but not always, so for those, the challenges will be greater). In this last decade or so of working, there must be a high priority placed on building anywhere from one year's living expenses saved to up to two years (having three years' expenses in the bank can be challenging, so it depends on how strongly you feel and your personal situation).

There is a strong reason for this, and if you understand this, you will be more motivated to insulate yourself by building this up.

The Story of Two Investors

Let's take a look at two investors at retirement time (see chart below). Both retired with $1,000,000 in their investment portfolio. And their monies were 100% invested in the S&P 500 and they were taking 10% withdrawals to start and increasing that 3% per year. (As a side note, this is not a prudent approach in terms of diversification, and this is taking an excessive percentage out, so this is for illustrative purposes only and not a strategy to mimic at all). [6]

Anyway, Investor A retired in 1973 ... the start of a two-year bear (down) market. What happens to the money is it runs out in nine years. Between taking monies out and losing, the declines are so large, the account can't handle both negatives. Investor B retired in 1982, the start of a long bull market. This portfolio lasts decades. After 20-plus years of taking an increased annual amount, there are now millions in the account. Investor B, over time, will have taken a few million and still have more to go, possibly never running out.

The first question that comes to mind is, was B smarter than A? No, not at all. They both had the same amount of money, took the same amount out (to start), inflated it the same ... just one was lucky to retire at the start of a long bull (up) market and the other started at the beginning of a bear (down) market. Those early downs adversely (and tremendously) affected the overall success, or lack thereof. The

---

6   The hypothetical case study results are for illustrative purposes only and should not be deemed a representation of past or future results. This example does not represent any specific product, nor does it reflect sales charges or other expenses that may be required for some investments. No representation is made as to the accurateness of the analysis. The S&P 500 Index is an unmanaged group of securities considered to be representative of the stock market in general. You cannot directly invest in the index.

key point of this is that sequence of returns during accumulation makes no difference, but the sequence of returns during retirement makes a huge difference. If the loss comes early in retirement, it will adversely and dramatically affect your values thereafter, as you are taking monies out. So, to better insulate, to prepare, having these savings set aside to "combat" this possibility is a sound strategy.

The point of this is you do not want to have the success of your retirement based on luck the year you retire. Since we can't predict the market the year we retire, the best way to insulate is to have a bucket of money not tied to the market. And if the year you retire, is a down period, then consider using your savings instead of pulling monies out of the market when it is going down. By having two years of living expenses sitting on the sideline, you are able to use an entire year of savings and still have one year in reserve. This also allows a little time for the market to rebound, so you are not decreasing your account via withdrawals and losses. If you planned on retiring in 2020, what we saw was a big, steep drop the end of the first quarter and into the second quarter because of Covid-19. If we had the insulation of this savings, we wouldn't have to withdraw monies from the market while it was down. In this particular point in time, the markets shot back up rather quickly. Certainly, time will tell if there is another deep drop from this pandemic but the security of savings will help the situation out.

These strategies of savings during the decades before and leading up to retirement are the backbone of your financial equation. It might be the least exciting element, but it is as critical as any other part of the equation. A weak link here will snowball into taking on more debt elsewhere. Sustained and plentiful debt is a recipe for struggle, so embrace having a healthy savings account(s) and build them up accordingly.

Will a Successful Retirement Depend Upon the Year You Retire?

#	Year	Investor A Beg Balance	Amount W/D	Ending Balance	S&P 500	#	Year	Investor B Beg Balance	Amount W/D	Ending Balance
1	1973	$1,000,000	$100,000	$767,700	-14.70%					
2	1974	$767,700	$103,000	$488,555	-26.50%					
3	1975	$488,555	$106,090	$524,741	37.20%					
4	1976	$524,741	$109,273	$514,766	23.90%					
5	1977	$514,766	$112,551	$373,255	-7.20%					
6	1978	$373,255	$115,927	$274,311	6.50%					
7	1979	$274,311	$119,405	$183,784	18.61%					
8	1980	$183,784	$122,987	$80,490	32.50%					
9	1981	$80,490	You are broke!		-4.92%					
10	1982				21.55%	1	1982	$1,000,000	$100,000	$1,093,950
11	1983		Total Withdrawn: $889,234		22.56%	2	1983	$1,093,950	$103,000	$1,214,508
12	1984				6.27%	3	1984	$1,214,508	$106,090	$1,177,916
13	1985				31.73%	4	1985	$1,177,916	$109,273	$1,407,724
14	1986				18.67%	5	1986	$1,407,724	$112,551	$1,536,982
15	1987				5.25%	6	1987	$1,536,982	$115,927	$1,495,660
16	1988				16.61%	7	1988	$1,495,660	$119,405	$1,604,851
17	1989				31.69%	8	1989	$1,604,851	$122,987	$1,951,466
18	1990				-3.11%	9	1990	$1,951,466	$126,667	$1,768,038
19	1991				30.37%	10	1991	$1,768,038	$130,477	$2,136,525
20	1992				7.62%	11	1992	$2,136,525	$134,392	$2,154,696
21	1993				10.08%	12	1993	$2,154,696	$138,423	$2,219,513
22	1994				1.32%	13	1994	$2,219,513	$142,576	$2,104,352
23	1995				37.58%	14	1995	$2,104,352	$146,853	$2,693,127
24	1996				22.96%	15	1996	$2,693,127	$151,259	$3,125,481
25	1997				33.36%	16	1997	$3,125,481	$155,797	$3,960,371
26	1998				28.58%	17	1998	$3,960,371	$160,471	$4,885,912
27	1999				21.04%	18	1999	$4,885,912	$165,285	$5,713,847
28	2000				-9.10%	19	2000	$5,713,847	$170,243	$5,039,136
29	2001				-11.89%	20	2001	$5,039,136	$175,351	$4,285,481
30	2002				-22.10%	21	2002	$4,285,481	$180,611	$3,197,694
31	2003				28.68%	22	2003	$3,197,694	$186,029	$3,875,410
32	2004				10.88%	23	2004	$3,875,410	$191,610	$4,084,597
33	2005				4.91%	24	2005	$4,084,597	$197,359	$4,078,101
					15.79%	25	2006	$4,078,101	$203,279	$4,486,656
					5.49%	26	2007	$4,486,656	$209,378	$4,512,101
					-37.00%	27	2008	$4,512,101	$215,659	$2,706,758
					26.46%	28	2009	$2,706,758	$222,129	$3,142,062
					15.06%	29	2010	$3,142,062	$228,793	$3,352,007
					2.11%	30	2011	$3,352,007	$235,657	$3,773,900
					16.00%	31	2012	$3,773,900	$242,726	$4,096,161
					32.39%	32	2013	$4,096,161	$250,008	$5,091,923
					13.69%	33	2014	$5,091,923	$257,508	$5,496,246
					1.40%	34	2015	$5,496,246	$265,234	$5,963,354
					11.96%	35	2016	$5,963,354	$273,191	$6,370,706
					21.83%	36	2017	$6,370,706	$281,386	$7,418,619
					-4.38%	37	2018	$7,418,619	$289,828	$6,816,549
						38	2019	$6,816,549	$298,523	
						39	2020	$ -		

Total Withdrawn → $6,915,935

Total Withdrawn so far ~: $7,000,000 (with almost $7,000,000 still left)

How We View Money

In addition to the various savings strategies, let's also look at money and how we view it when spending it. We often assign varying values, so maybe if we better understand it, we might be better at holding onto it.

How we look at money, how we spend it and how we hold it, will vary according to our perception of it. For example, if an item cost $2,000, the perception of that cost would seem greater if we were paying in cash, slightly lower (or less painful) if we wrote a check or used a debit card, slightly less painful if we charged it, and almost painless if we financed it (say $111 for 18 months interest-free). To stand at the register and part with twenty $100 bills or forty $50 bills would make that buyer cringe a bit. Cash seems to carry most weight.

Pulling out the credit card is so easy in society today, and we do it almost every day. We rarely grasp how much we are spending until you get your bill in the mail. That pit in your stomach is then trying to figure out how to pay off that bill that month. For many, it will happen two or three times a month because we have more than one credit card. Digging that hole is so easy. The temptation to not pay it off in full, or the inability to, means that going into debt becomes reality and thus, the cycle begins. And if what you charge during the new cycle of billing is greater than what you pay, you have gone down this road of dancing with the devil. The issue here is that today's purchase is not felt or seen or recognized for two or three weeks. So, the true cost is delayed a bit, long enough to be mostly out of sight.

We will better serve our long-term selves if we are in tune with how to effectively manage money. If we are able to restrain the uses of easier methods of spending, then that dollar not spent is essentially a dollar saved.

Of course, if we need to access items like interest-free financing to make larger purchases easier on our budget, this is effective. But buyer beware, this becomes habit-forming and one can purchase big screen televisions, sun rooms, roofs, appliances and more like this and before you know it, your monthly costs have gone through the roof (the one you just financed over 3 years). These payment options do make it easy … maybe sometimes too easy, and we become collectors of monthly payments.

Find Ways Not to Spend

There are those that have to get designer coffee every morning. They frequent certain stores and often pay up to $5 or $6 for a cup of coffee. Done daily, this adds up to maybe $25 a week and over a month that is over $100. These stores incentivize you to keep coming back, making purchases easier with apps and rewards programs. Money can fly out of the wallet fast. This is also assuming you don't make any other purchases while at the counter, and we all know that muffin is calling your name. I'm not saying eliminate this little luxury you afford yourself, but what I am saying is pay attention. Maybe some days, you refrain from buying the coffee and make it from home.

For most of us, money is finite and limited. Where, how often and how much we spend it can be unlimited. We are best served in finding little ways to curtail spending, finding these creative methods of savings and the result will be more kept dollars. That is the reward.

A Point about Debt

Overspending or ill-advised spending will often lead to racking up credit card debt. Beware. That is a dangerous road to travel and one that is steep to come back from, so you will want to avoid at all costs going down that road if you can.

If you are in this predicament prior to reading this book, then your first and foremost focus must be on reducing the debt and eventually eliminating the bad debt. You can have a mortgage and a car payment, even student loans, but you must learn to live paying off credit cards monthly.

Overspending and not saving money is common today. If we can implement some of the strategies as discussed, we stand a better chance of success. In the next chapter, we will look at investing and markets; a topic that consumers are more inclined to focus on. But do not ignore this foundation of your financial world. Savings is a key component.

Savings in Summary

Preparation, segmentation, discipline, and prudence become the keys here. If we can prepare in advance for both the visible items that we see and the hidden ones that for sure will pop up, then we can avoid that collection of multiple loans and inflated credit card bills.

But it will require discipline and foresight. As well as holding off on some purchases. Too often today, we buy things to replace things that are still effective, operational, or useful. But we wanted the latest style, a newer version, a larger whatever. And we justify that it's only a small monthly cost. So, we have to learn that that thinking is dangerous.

Action Items:

- First, let's determine what your Pure Savings and Put & Take account levels are. What are your monthly expenses? Start with three months' expenses in the Pure Savings. For the time being, start with between $2,000 and $3,000 of P & T. Determine how long it will take to get to those levels.
- When you have those two accounts set up (they don't have to be fully funded yet), then open the "house / vacation" account. Let's start to get that savings going. The house account can be for someone who doesn't own yet, but wants to eventually buy, or it can be for someone who does own but is preparing for that next upgrade.

- Start your $5 bill game. Put a cup in your closet, and during the course of your week, pull out the $5 bills you get and fill the cup. Watch it grow.

CHAPTER 7

Investing in Equity Markets and Historical Perspective

"Misperception of risk—overestimating the risk of holding equities. The other far more insidious mistake is underestimating the risk of not holding them. The real long-term risk of equities is not owning them."

Nick Murray

I want to limit this chapter to the conversation of investing in equity markets, in stock markets. This is about providing perspective, past results, where those numbers fit in the conversation and why it is so important to understand in terms of your planning. This is not about giving you the answers of what to invest in, nor is this chapter about exploring various other investment opportunities or solutions. There are countless options, strategies, platforms, methods and more, but for purposes of this conversation, we are going to limit it to the broad equity markets.

If we recognize that savings is about liquidity and not about performance, then investing is about growth (and possibly income, depending on your goals) and liquidity is secondary. We must have both savings and investments, both liquidity and growth opportunities. Both offer something to the overall solution, so ignoring one of them will come at a great cost.

There is a long history of equity markets that we can extract tremendous information from that can really serve us as investors. To better understand is to be better positioned to make better decisions. Think about it in terms of professional gambling. The popularity of tournament poker has exploded in the last ten years. There have been many books written on the topic of how to be a better player. Professionals and the better amateurs understand these odds and play their cards to maximize their hands. Many amateurs tend to be less informed, thus they tend to make more mistakes. Amateurs often play from emotion and the "gut" because they don't know the statistics and odds. Professionals know these statistics and more often play their cards trying the get the best of the odds. They tend to be less emotional.

Investing has similar qualities and characteristics . More informed investors tend to understand the rich history and tend to know when the odds favor them. As a result, they tend to have greater long-term real-life results. Amateurs tend NOT TO. Amateur investors often act on emotion.

Let's take a look at one particular market index because we will reference this often, which is the Standard and Poors 500 (S&P 500). It was originally called the Composite Index in 1923 and expanded to 90 stocks in 1926. It wasn't until 1957 that it expanded to 500 stocks.

Having an understanding of the past will potentially guide us in our decision-making. Of course, it does not assure anything, but it does tell a story that to ignore would be shameful. From 1926 through 2019, there are 94 calendar years. And in those 94 years, there have been 69 years that have been positive, leaving 25 years that were negative. That means, 73% of years have been up and 27% that were down. Not a bad percentage in terms of gains versus losses. But people, do not invest for a one-year period, so let's establish that investing is for a longer period of time. If you have a need for money in three or even five years' time, then savings might better serve you. Investing presents opportunities for growth, but you expose your monies to volatility, meaning that you could see markets drop and if you needed to take said monies out of the market, then you might experience a loss. Savings solutions do not expose you to a downside, but the cost is that you have limited opportunities to grow your money.

But let's fast forward in terms of holding periods. Let's move past five years, past ten and settle on a 20-year period. More specifically, all the 20-year periods from 1926–2019. There are 75 rolling 20-year horizons: 1926–1945, 1927–1946, 1928–1947 and so on. Of those 75, 100% of them have recorded positive returns from the S&P 500, meaning 0% have ever had a negative performance. Not one single 20-year horizon has ever lost. Pick one starting with a bear market (a bear market is where the index falls 20%) or pick one ending with a bear. Pick a period with more than one bear … you get the same result in terms of up versus down: a positive return. Of course, you get different performance figures for those periods, but from a broad measure of positive or negative, they are all positive.

How Many Times Has the Broad Index Been Negative?

I want to highlight this point: there has never been a 20-year horizon on the broad domestic index that has ever had a losing or down period. Never. There is a quote later in this chapter that mentions creating a loss in a well-diversified portfolio is a "manmade achievement," this is what that is referring to. That to create a loss, an investor would have had to sell out typically when the market dropped making that drop permanent, when, all they had to do was nothing and just stay the course, because markets have always come back.

Consider this thought, losing money in the stock market is not something the market has delivered, it is something that is created by the investor. If one diversifies and stays in the market long term, history says loud and clear that you always "win" (although using diversification as part of your investment strategy neither assures nor guarantees better performance and cannon protect against loss of principal due to changing market conditions). Keep in mind, this is using the broad index as the investment solution, not a single stock. Of course, single stocks have lost, many businesses have stopped trading, but the theory of diversifying comes into play here and offers that insulation that buying single stocks does not offer.

We were "taught" that the stock market was risky, but a diversified portfolio over a long period tells us something different, so how we define risk needs to change. Risk needs to be defined as not reaching your goals, not defined as a stock market drop. Risk is not meeting the dollars you need later in life.

You have a choice in your investing life and that is to expose your portfolio to volatility on the front end of investing so you can accumulate enough resources to outlive you on the back end OR don't participate in equity markets (that have a long, rich tradition of growth) and you may get to your golden years with an inadequate nest egg that you may outlive. Which of these scenarios do you want to happen? Avoid equity investing long term with the possibility of outliving your monies, or have equities be a part of your portfolio and accept the short term volatility so that you have the potential of greater dollars in those retirement years. Can't have both, you must pick one.

Interesting Set of Numbers

Over the last 50 years, if the following four percentages were loss rates, what option would you choose between A – 50%, B – 35%, C – 25% or D – 15%? The answer is obvious, correct? D. If they all had the same timeframe, which option would you choose now? Again, quite obvious, stay with D. These four choices correspond with HOW OFTEN you look at your portfolio, "A" being daily, "B" being monthly, "C" quarterly, and "D" annually. These are ALL the same investment portfolio, the S&P 500, just differing in how often you LOOK at them! As you can clearly see, the longer the time frame, the greater the possibility of having gains. And as expressed prior, if we extend the years of investing, the story gets even better. Odds are enhanced the longer we stay invested.

The media won't point this out when markets drop. They tell you the "here and now" that markets are dropping and oftentimes suggest you get out, or tell you how ineffective 401(k)s are, or how markets are failing the investing consumer. I have rarely seen articles that stress this long horizon to calm the investor.

Looking at a Recent Bear

Let's take a look at one of the most recent drops in the market, the 2007–2008 bear market. The S&P 500 was at roughly 1,500 and it dropped below 700. This was a near 60% drop in the broad market. Devastating. I suspect investors bailed out when the market dropped below 1,000 and it kept going lower. Panic and fear set in and more got out as the market sunk below 800. And it kept going down. Those that got out made their losses permanent.

Let me remind you of where the market is at the start of 2020: over 3,200. Then we came upon another "bear" caused by Covid-19 that pushed the market back down to the 2,800 level. All one had to do back in the 2007–2008 free fall was refrain from acting on their emotions (and do nothing). The same applies in 2020. I don't say it is easy. Doing nothing is not easy in life, but investing requires you to be counter to your emotions.

Another drop in the market occurred the last quarter of 2018 when the market fell 19.8%. This did not hit bear territory but came as close as it can get. The thing to consider is, did those 500 companies really lose 20% of their value in the space of those 100 days? These are 500 mature, well-financed companies that are collectively doing very well, so does the volatility of the market determine long-term value or do the collective pieces tell the story? One of the problems with declining markets is investor panic and emotions that lead to selling, and that reaction leads to more investors following suit. This herd mentality leads to lower prices, not because the company is doing poorly necessarily. When pessimism reigns, irrationality follows.

A Study

There is a study done annually by Dalbar and it shows the gap between what investors earn over a 20-year horizon and what the broad index has earned.

For example, the 20-year horizon in the late 1990s and early 2000s, the average return of the S&P 500 was in the mid to high teens. The average equity fund investor in those years ranged from 3 to 7%. The gap was over 10%. This was for a 20-year period, mind you. That difference has dropped, and the gap has closed, but it seems to have leveled out around a 4% spread (between what investors earn and what the S&P 500 earns). This is still a huge figure over 20 years.

This is determined by the flow of money in and out of funds. Rolling time periods show that in every single one of them, the market has done better than what individuals do. And the reasons why are mainly tied to emotions. When markets go up, investors get excited, feel good, and it shows in the flow of money: they invest more. Then, as markets do, they go down, they decline, they fall. And investor emotions panic and fear. They move their money OUT of the equity investments. They put that money in the bank. They stop adding to their portfolio or cut back investing. The thought is: "I'm losing money" or "I don't want to throw good money after bad." Quite common.

Let's review for a moment here. Investors were buying high in the stock market and then selling low, doing the wrong thing at the worst possible time. This is why investors always underperform markets. Invariably, markets go back up, yet investors routinely get out. (Please allow me to remind you the percentage of times markets have had positive returns over 20-year periods, that percentage is 100%). As Pogo Possum said, "We have seen the enemy and it is us." We tend to be our own worst enemy. Investing is emotional and as emotional beings; we are wired to fail. We can't get out of our own way. Understand that the seeds of upward trends are sown in these down markets. And the opposite is also true in that, during these long periods of upward trends, the seeds of a dip or drop are germinating. But history shows that the ups are longer and steeper, so since we can't readily "time" these events, staying the course is often the best plan of action.

Interesting thoughts from others on the topic:

"For many of us, the single greatest obstacle to the pursuit of investment success is our own proclivity to panic. The dominant determinant to real life outcomes has more to do with investor behavior and less to do with investment performance. The enemy of successful investing is human emotion."

Nick Murray

"The key to making money in stocks is not to be scared out of them."

Peter Lynch

"Fear has a greater grasp on human action than does the impressive weight of historical performance."

Jeremy Seigel

"Far more money has been lost by investors preparing for corrections or trying to anticipate corrections than has been lost in corrections themselves."

Peter Lynch

"Don't just do something, stand there."

Louis Rukeyser

"The stock market is a highly efficient mechanism for the transfer of wealth from the impatient investor to the patient."

Warren Buffet

"Permanent loss in a well-diversified equity portfolio is always a human achievement of which the market is incapable."

Nick Murray

"Your success in investing will depend in part on your character and guts and in part on your ability to realize at the height of ebullience and the depth of despair alike, this too shall pass."

Jack Bogle

"If you want the kinds of returns that equities have historically provided, you must accept the kinds of gut-wrenching declines which the equity markets have historically experienced. It's a package deal. The longer your time horizon, the less stock market volatility affects you."

Nick Murray

"Faith has been rewarded and pessimism punished. Optimism is historically the only realism – the only worldview that squares with the facts and with the historical record."

Nick Murray

"There is simply no escaping the fact that managing human behavior is the keystone to being a successful investor. No level of investment skill, which is rare on its own, is sufficient to overcome the cancer of bad behavior."

Dr. Daniel Crosby

"Never underestimate the power of doing nothing."

Winnie-the-Pooh

"Successful investing requires patience that is measured in years, not weeks. It is boring."

Charlie Epstein

"History provides a crucial insight regarding market crises: they are inevitable, painful and ultimately, surmountable."

Shelby Davis

"In the short run, the market is a voting machine. In the long run, it is a weighing machine."

Benjamin Graham

"Dreams will not be thwarted, faith will be rewarded."

Bruce Springsteen

"The stock market is weird—every time one person sells, another one buys. And they both think they're smart."

Anonymous

"You've got to go out on a limb sometimes because that is where the fruit it."

Will Rogers

A Picture Is Worth a 1,000 Words

When we look at returns on this broad index for one year from 1950 to today, we find that variance can be large. The high for a calendar year has exceeded 40% and the low has been close to a 40% loss, so that gap is 80%. But let's look at the 5-, 10- and 20-year figures and something very interesting happens. The gap shrinks and as noted prior, the worst 20-year return is positive. The bar is north of the zero line (see chart below by JP Morgan).

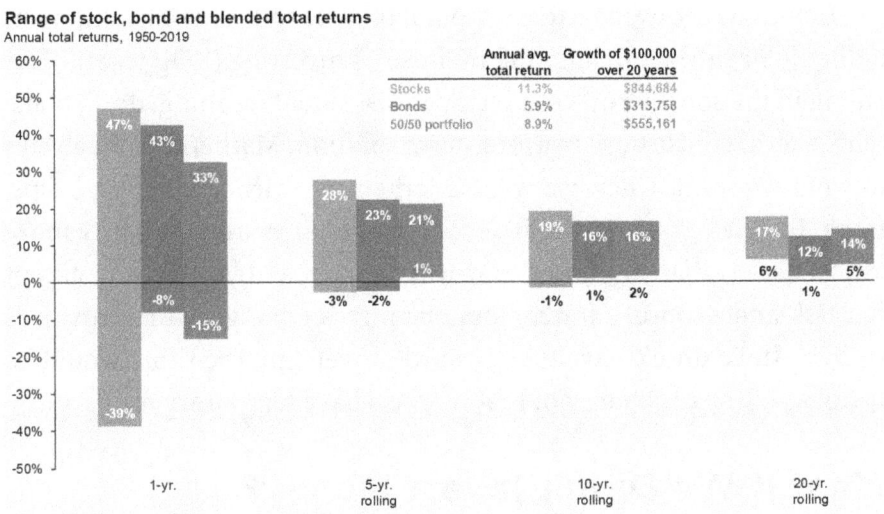

Understand Your Horizon

As an investor, we must understand our timeline, our horizon for the monies being invested. If we need the monies for a down payment on a house we are buying in two years, then that is set in stone. If we need money for our kids' college education and they are in tenth grade, then we know exactly the time frame. And if we are investing for our retirement, we might have an idea of when we'd like to retire. So, for example, if you are 40 years old, you have roughly 25 years to retirement, but keep in mind, unlike being at a casino when you cash your chips out when you're done, you don't then cash your investments at retirement time. You may have another two, three or even four decades IN retirement, so we still need our investment to grow. We need to stay invested, maybe we alter the allocation, but that is a different conversation. Staying on point here, money needs to be invested for the 25 years "to" retirement, plus another possible 30 "in."

Let me remind the reader how many times the broad index has declined over long periods. Zero. If one is the loneliest number, then in this context, zero is also the most beautiful number.

Emotions throw investors off, but if they stepped back for a moment and let their horizon match the premise of investing (long term), then bailing in the short term would happen less often: meaning, don't make a short-term conclusion on a long-term solution. Markets do not always do what we want, when we want. Markets experience gyrations, dips, drops, fluctuations, and the like. But it doesn't matter. What is more critical here is that you know they will happen, and you have to accept that risk and exposure for the opportunity for the growth. Growth is survival. If we didn't have that upward movement, then that would be the focus of the problem, not that markets have temporary drops.

What If We Didn't Invest Money?

Let's spend a moment on building your long-term nest egg through cash. Let's say the vehicle you chose to park your money was purely cash, so you didn't invest it. There were no earnings, but you rationalized that you were not going to take hits. You've heard the horror stories, you read the articles about crashes, your friends have told you they "lost their shirts" at times, so you've decided to not play that game.

Here are a few variables in this scenario. You are 30, you want to retire at 65, you can save $10,000 a year for 15 years, $20,000 a year for the last 20 years. That means, that over the 35 years of accumulation, you were able to save $550,000. Let's also assume that you will need money for 30 years into retirement. Of course, one never really knows exactly what that time frame is but for our example here we'll run with that. The $550,000 might seem like a lot of money (and it is) but in terms of supporting you over that 30-year horizon, you will find that will be woefully short.

Let's examine for starters, the rising costs of goods. If we use the historic rate of rising costs of goods, then we are looking at 3%. Some items will rise at a faster rate, while some items like technology have actually fallen, but most items have gone up in price. So, a loaf of bread that is $5 today will be upwards to $9 at retirement time in the example above.

Or to put it in a different light, a $1,000,000 portfolio value today will be approximately about 50% of its value in 30 years, so the spending power will be about $500,000 in over three decades. So, the $550,000 that was saved has a spending equivalent of about $275,000. Ask yourself if you take your retirement income from this bucket, is this the lifestyle you want?

Let's Redefine Risk

When we talk about risk, we too often associate risk with market declines. But pay attention to this example because this is where risk lies: you won't have nearly enough money. Guaranteed. The risk to be evaluated is not of owning stocks but of NOT owning them.

Read this last sentence one more time.

Let's consider one other point in the conversation. As we need the money to last possibly three decades, the idea is not to take money out too fast. If we skim 5% per year, we run the risk of spending down the principal but running with that figure, a $1,000,000 portfolio throws off then, $50,000 a year. Keep in mind, for most people, these portfolios are retirement accounts, and most will be taxed at an ordinary income rate, so that $50,000 is a gross number. The net now becomes about $35,000.

Going back to our savings example (where we didn't invest the money), using the saved amount (not the purchasing power amount), at $550,000, taking 5%, equates to $27,500. The good news here is, because it is in cash, there is no tax to this equation. If you are literally just taking $100 bills from your stack, in this example, that is not taxed as ordinary income. This example is making the assumption you did not invest these dollars in a retirement plan. If you did invest money in a retirement plan but used the money market as the investment vehicle (so as not to assume equity market risk), then these dollars coming out will incur a tax.

But there is a fly in this ointment. You see, if you take 5% of the cash that is not growing, then this will last 20 installments, so at the end of 20 years, you have run out of money. You have not possibly run out of time. Every single "dip into that bucket" of money is lowering the amount, eventually to zero. Again, I want to emphasize this point, you have run out of money but not time. **This is the very problem we are trying to solve.**

If your scenario is that you will run out of money, the question is then what?

The problem is not the broad, well-diversified public companies that make up an index where we can park our money. The problem is not that markets rise and fall, ebb and flow all on an inclining path. The problem is, we need money later in life for decades and having our money grow is a necessity, not a luxury. We can't afford to let it sit idle. We can't allow ourselves to think that investing in some of the great companies is the risk or problem. NOT investing is the problem. NOT investing is the risk. It's plain to see.

And we can't circumvent down markets. We must invest with them and through them. We can't time markets because we don't know when they will fall. No one has been able to predict them in spite of what you may read from time to time. If I predict every single year the market is going to crash, then technically, I can say I accurately predicted the market was going to drop, because I will be right eventually.

Let me sum up this point: it is not the risk of investing in the stock market that needs to be examined closely. It is the risk of NOT investing in the stock market that will critically reduce your chances of success.

What If We Did Invest Money?

Looking at that same example of investing $10,000 for 15 years and then $20,000 for the last 15 years and let's assume our investment growth rate was a flat 6%, how much will we have accumulated? You will have topped the $1,000,000 mark. You will have an account with over twice the amount, but let's not stop there. If we keep the money invested during the withdrawal period and you continue to earn roughly 5% or even 6%, and withdraw 5%, then your money will be able to last much longer than the example above. Keep in mind, every dollar you take in the cash example, you reduce your lump sum. In this example, you are essentially taking the earnings annually and keep the lump sum to stick around not only to support you but then to pass on to your kids or favorite charity.

Which plan would you rather select? Which option offers you a better long-term financial road to live?

Drops in the Market Can Be Your Friend

Going back to the broad index, let's look at some other numbers that tell an interesting story. The idea here is for you to have a greater understanding of what the market has done and even with these points, it has risen steadily and consistently over decades. The following chart shows from 1980 the average intra year decline on the index. Meaning, at some point during the year, the index has fallen.

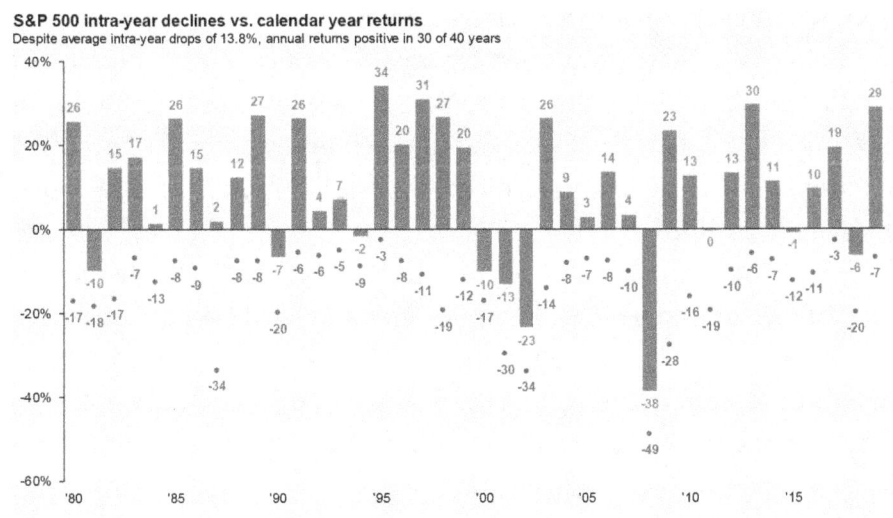

As you can see, every year, there are dips and drops, even in the up years. The average drop is 14%. Yes, that is correct, the average drop since 1980 is 14%. This is not the same as the average loss in the calendar year. Keep in mind, since 1980, there have been only nine years the S&P 500 index has lost for the entire year. But this chart is showing an intra year figure.

So, to manage your expectations, you need to know that if you're investing in equity portfolios, you will incur drops every year. Prognosticators that tell us that the market will drop 10% or even 20% are not telling us anything that doesn't happen regularly. That would be like me saying we are going to get some rain in April, and we are going to get a scorcher in August. Now, if I was going to predict we were going to get a snowstorm in August, THAT would be bold. That would be a prediction.

A Recent History of Bear Markets

The term "bull and bear markets" are tossed around often in investing circles. They define movements of the broad index, so bear markets are when the markets fall 20% or more, and bull markets are when the markets rise 20% or more. Looking back, we are able to see exact dates when we enter and exit these periods of time.

Below is a chart of all the bear markets since World War II. In addition to the roughly dozen listed, there are also three examples in this time period that the market did not technically enter a bear market but came really close. The most recent was the last quarter of 2018, when the market dropped 19.8%.

Please note, this maybe be considered "risk" but pay attention to the performance figures three months after and twelve months after the bottom and you begin to realize, these periods are not risk, they are just periods of volatility. Understand the distinction between the two. Risk is defined as the potential loss. If you sold your equity shares during these periods, then that loss would be made permanent, or realized. If you did

NOTHING and let the market work itself out, then see what happens after those bear market figures?

What most likely escapes you, dear reader, is that since the mid-1950s with over a dozen of these deep drops, the market has gone from the high teens to over 3,000. And keep in mind, this is just the price of the S&P 500; this does not include the annual dividend this index pays out, which is roughly an additional 2%.

So, I have a suggestion that is rather simple for those that have money invested in equity markets. Stay the course. I didn't say it was easy, but it is simple. In the words of a famous philosopher, Winnie the Pooh, "never underestimate the power of doing nothing."

What is most difficult is the emotional side of "it." When you see markets drop and you will, you will want to act or react in these moments. But this is the worst thing you can do, history says. You have the rich and long history to look upon to help ease the emotional pain you are feeling. As Tom Petty expressed, "Waiting is the Hardest Part."

Dates of Market Peak	Dates of Market Trough	% Return	Duration	Market Peak S&P	Market Trough S&P	3 Months after low	12 Months after low
05/29/46	06/13/49	-30%	36.5 months	19.3	13.6	18.17%	52.74%
08/02/56	10/22/57	-22%	14.5 months	49.7	39.1	6.91%	36.30%
12/12/61	06/26/62	-28%	6.5 months	72.6	52.3	8.27%	37.42%
02/09/66	10/07/66	-22%	8.0 months	94.1	73.2	13.38%	37.34%
11/29/68	05/26/70	-36%	18.0 months	108.4	69.3	18.41%	48.96%
01/11/73	10/03/74	-48%	20.5 months	120.2	62.3	15.08%	44.43%
09/21/76	03/06/78	-19%	17.5 months	107.8	86.9	12.21%	23.31%
11/28/80	08/12/82	-27%	20.5 months	140.5	102.4	38.14%	66.11%
08/25/87	12/24/87	-34%	4.0 months	336.8	223.9	20.44%	25.92%
07/16/90	10/11/90	-20%	3.0 months	369.1	295.5	7.73%	33.55%
07/17/98	08/31/98	-19%	1.5 months	1186.8	957.3	22.02%	39.81%
03/24/00	10/09/02	-49%	30.5 months	1527.5	776.7	19.98%	36.15%
10/09/07	03/09/09	-57%	17.0 months	1565.1	676.5	40.01%	63.03%
09/20/18	12/26/18	-19.8%	3.0 months	2940.91	2356.48	19.61%	36.80%
02/19/20	03/23/20	-34%	1 month	3,386	2,237	40.63%	

Investing is often done in two forms: a one-time investment or over regular periods. You may roll monies over or inherit monies and this is done as a one-time deposit. Retirement planning is done as a regular ongoing method and when this is happening, this is actually the best time to be investing, during these downturns. This is where you get your leverage in the market. This is the moment in time that when people bail, the studies reflect where investors underperform markets time and time again, this is why. They miss out on the "best part": buying at a discount. As investors, we look at dips and drops as a problem when we should be looking at them as the complete opposite.

When markets decline, think about the headlines and articles you will see. You will see themes like, "Investors losing money in the 401(k)s", or "Retirement Monies at Risk." You know exactly what I am referencing, the media focus is on the down in the moment. Consumers never see articles that encourage staying the course or information about the long rich history of the market.

When markets decline, oftentimes it is because of a wide spectrum of reasons; for example, a housing bubble or a tech bubble, or most recently, a worldwide pandemic. In many of these situations, that actual value of the underlying company did not necessarily drop in value because of the situation, even though the stock price did because of the market decline. The expression "low tide sinks all boats" comes to mind. When the general direction of the market is going down, that does not mean that all companies' profits and revenues are following suit. The dollar cost averaging during these down cycles oftentimes will pay off for well-run companies when overall market directions swing back up.

But you will now know better, having read to this point in the book. You will know now that these drops are your friend, these are the small turbo boosts over time, these are accelerators over the course of your accumulation years. When you have between 30 and 40 years to accumulate your retirement nest egg, you will need to come to expect that you might encounter, say four or five of these moments in your investing life. And this does not even count the market corrections that come along more frequently (they tend to be 10% drops whereas bears are 20% losses).

When I reference the point of drops be your friend, if you are adding to your investments regularly, then this is called "dollar cost averaging." So, for example, you might be contributing $200 of monthly pay or 5% per pay to your retirement plan. When the price of a stock drops (during these periods), that means your investment contribution will buy a greater number of shares.

To oversimplify, if you are investing $100 every period and a fund is priced at $50, then in that period, you purchased two shares. The idea leading up to retirement is to be an accumulator of shares. When the market falls and your fund or stock drops to $25, this is where the emotion comes to the surface. You see your stock price cut in half and too often, this is where investors decide to bail. But if you continue buying, you will have purchased four shares this period, so when that fund or stock rises again, above $50, you will have purchased some shares at much lower prices, hence your leverage. This is where investors get their return. But you have to stay in, you have to be buying at those dips and drops.

The key is to manage your expectations and emotions. If you understand markets rise and fall, maybe your perspective will dramatically change. So, learn the power of doing nothing. Understand the big picture, the long horizon, and what markets have done. Understand that corrections and deep drops happen. Sometimes they are fast, sometimes, they drag out. Again, the ones that drag out, these are wonderful buying opportunities, so embrace them. Welcome them with open arms.

Of course, if your holding period "to" retirement is shorter and a deep drop is upon us, then that is where a healthy savings account insulates us. If you decide to retire in the same year as a bear, then planning and forethought will prove to be valuable to increasing the odds of your success. It is quite possible that you could be planning to step back, and it so happens it is in a time like 2007–08. The market dropping is not the problem. The problem is that we don't readily want to take liquidations when the market is experiencing those moments, so this goes back to the savings chapter and the strategies discussed there.

One other point, when you are closer to retirement (let's assume you have about 5 years left of working/investing but have a large retirement account and are also still investing), one strategy you can employ is to move the lump sum to a portfolio that offers less volatility. So, for example, if your current stock to bond allocation is 80/20, then you could "dial down" to a 60/40. But for the new money being invested annually, you could dial that up to 100/0, so that a smaller pot of money can take advantage of drops by buying low but the larger pot of money would be insulated a bit more.

Action Items:

- Take a look back at your investing history and make note of what you did, when you did it and why. And see if those actions were beneficial in the long run or if they were detrimental to your long-term growth. Meaning, did you stop investing in the last draw down? Or did you panic and sell holdings?

- Take note of where investing is in your priorities. Have you flatlined in terms of how much you have been investing the last 5, 10 or even 20 years? Have you spent more on other items but not your retirement nest egg? Explore how you can max out in your retirement plan (not max out to the match, but max out to the limits you can invest in the plan).

- Talk to some family members willing to share what they did and why. Maybe this is a moment that you can learn from someone else's mistakes. This is not for you to point out what they did wrong but for you to see in "real life" situations, what could have been different for your parents or grandparents. Gaining perspective might alter your path. If a family member is in their eighties or nineties, inquire if they saved enough. Did they save at all? What would they have done differently? What experience did they have in equity markets? Maybe there are nuggets there for the taking, but it might not be in what they did; it might be more in what they didn't do, and they might not realize it.

CHAPTER 8

Just Sign Up

"Most people have the will to succeed but they don't have the will to prepare to succeed."

"Bear" Bryant

Using analogies, examples, and stories allow us to better see and understand a situation more clearly. We love to give examples of sports stories or athletes because we often identify with them in some way. We know who is having a great year. We know who the greatest athletes from each sport are (or we can debate it comparing athletes across generations). Almost all sports and players have statistics and metrics we can regurgitate and/or examine in some form, from home runs, to wins, to number of majors, to rushing yards, to how many gold medals, and so on.

So, what does it take to be successful in a sport? Of course, success is a broad term, but for this conversation, let's define success as rising to professional level. To play professionally in most any sport, you must put your time in to practice. There is no substitute for hard work. There is a correlation between time spent working on your craft or skills and results.

Practice doesn't assure results, but it certainly increases the odds of success. Most amateurs aren't willing to put the time in to drill in the actions or movements to enhance their game. There are few who are naturally gifted, of course, but that only goes so far and for so few. To get ahead, one has to hire coaches and work hard to rise from mediocrity to potential success. Behind the scenes, we don't see how they keep their bodies in peak condition or the reps they put in or the stress they are under. We just see the results of their work.

We have witnessed countless stories of how parents have pushed their kids to greatness. Two of the more famous stories are Tiger Woods and the Williams sisters. These kids were groomed for greatness and they all rose to the highest levels in their respective sports. Make no mistake, their work ethic was beyond the norm and they started at very young ages. Success is the result of many things coming together, but the foundation is hard work.

The same is true of our careers. In our society, if you want to enter certain occupations, you may need to earn a degree, pass additional exams or complete a number of years in residency. You just can't "decide" to become an engineer or physician or attorney or electrician by declaring it. One can't just read law books and declare you are an attorney. To earn these rights, one will need to study, possibly take a review course, spend hours of preparation, take practices tests, possibly hire a tutor and more.

Success in some fields is often results oriented. Many career positions will measure success from a list that includes sales, commissions, revenues, clients, patients, completion, managing, documenting, recording, analyzing, distributing, organizing, allocating and more. But in almost any scenario, the metric won't simply be "showing up." Imagine for a moment that all you had to do was show up for work. You didn't have to sell anything or meet a quota or learn the programs or understand what was in volumes of books or know the anatomy or determine where pain was coming from. No, you were paid handsomely with bonuses and raises for JUST SHOWING UP. We know this is not really the formula for success. Drive, determination, focus are some of the many attributes to being successful in the work environment. It's not just sports that has this variance of beginner to professional, but this same correlation can be made to many other aspects of life. There is playing an instrument at a high level but when one starts out, they are making noise. Anyone can make a burger on a grill, but the top of the game is often defined as being a chef. Most anyone can perform a self-working magic trick, but the best are highly skilled magicians trained in the art of illusion.

There are some exceptions to most every rule. There are some athletes that are naturally talented. There are some with innate artistic ability and probably never have taken lessons. Of course, there are some that are brilliant but to harness those smarts, I suspect they too pushed themselves in fields beyond their boundaries and increased their knowledge base. And financially, there are some that either inherited their wealth, won it, or married into it and they never really had to "work for it." But like the ones mentioned here, these are the few, the outliers, not the masses.

To reach these upper heights in all of these fields, occupations and positions, the common elements are hard work, practice, lessons, determination, drive, desire, overcoming obstacles … you know, the many qualities that define greatness. So, what does this have to do with financial independence and building your retirement portfolio?

What if I told you that you COULD be rewarded for just showing up when it comes to retirement planning?

The Best Feature of a 401(k) or 403(b)

If I were to ask you, "What is the BEST part of a 401(k)," what would your answer be? Take a moment here …

Welcome back. The traditional answers are the tax benefits or the company match. These are excellent benefits and certainly one could make a case they are the best. Some companies match upwards and beyond 10%, so that is a generous commitment to helping their people succeed in accumulating wealth. But these great benefits are secondary to one feature that is almost invisible and goes unnoticed.

The best part of a 401(k) is that it is the ONE investment that requires no effort. You don't have to have the ***discipline*** to be successful here. You just have to sign up through your employer. You just have to get in. Participate. That's all. Fill out the application to enter the plan and there is a question that says, "How much would you like to invest?" This is usually written in terms of percent or dollars. This is then sent off to the payroll company to take that amount out EVERY pay. You don't need to remind them; you don't need to confirm it each pay, it just happens. That simple. That's all. Crazy how easy that was. And the paycheck you get is then the NET figure of that deduction. All of those characteristics I described above to be great in these other fields and avocations are NOT necessary here to define success in building financial independence. THAT is the beauty here. Just sign up. Just get in … and defer money. No discipline required. Success is afforded to anyone wanting to join. Not an exclusive club. Take a moment here to let this point sink in.

Client Stories

In this chapter, I want to highlight the difference between two clients, Frank and Stephanie.

Frank is the owner of a small service business. Frank started off his career with another organization but eventually came into his father's business and then eventually took over. Frank does well, making up to $400,000. As Frank entered his sixties, we started working together to build a financial plan. We started our relationship when I took over his 401(k) plan, so I was able to meet his employees.

Stephanie is a multi-decade employee of the firm, has shown loyalty, and is also entering the tail end of her working life. She has risen to a level where the compensation for her role is at its maximum, and she makes roughly $75,000. From time to time, she received a year-end bonus of between $5,000 and $10,000.

Frank lives a good life. Drives a nice car, lives in a nice house, supports his kids, paying for their education and travels from time to time. He's married and the kids are now out of the house. Frank and his wife have a condo at the beach. They also belong to a golf club. Candidly, this sounds typical of some business owners.

Franks 401(k) balance was $325,000, and his wife had an IRA with roughly $175,000. They had little in savings and less than $60,000 in other investments. The value of the business, he felt approached $1,000,000, so his initial comments when we first started planning were centered around the bulk of his retirement would come from the sale of the business.

Stephanie, on the other hand, had no ownership. She started in the 401(k) plan the first year she was eligible, rolled some money over from her prior plan, and has never contributed less than 10%. In the years she got the larger bonuses, she would put 50% of bonus away, and she used the remaining amount on holiday shopping.

Stephanie was also married, owned her home (with 12 years left on the mortgage) and two kids who were out of the house. Stephanie has amassed $725,000 in her 401(k). She doesn't have a lot in savings or other investments, but between her 401(k) and her husband's, they have over $1,000,000 for their future.

The Irony

The scenario described above is quite a common. Meaning, what I see is from the very top group of income earners, there is usually one or two who have neglected their savings accounts. They have relied on their high income in the later years to think they will solve the problem, and oftentimes that isn't the case. They have lived a good life but have little to show for their success when they reach their sixties.

In their roster of employees, there is often a Stephanie who has diligently saved, year in year out. It wasn't always a lot, but it was done over decades. And in some years, a little more than planned was contributed via year-end bonuses. Nevertheless, the Stephanies, who never made more than $90,000 per year, are in a better financial position in terms of retirement accumulation. This particular Stephanie dedicated herself to being the best employee she could be but was never offered company stock and never rose to management level. But yet, here she was, holding one of the highest account balances in the plan.

Other high-paid executives also lacked the balance she held. To be fair, those others have not been in the plan as long as Stephanie, so maybe they do have larger account balances elsewhere, but this doesn't take away the success Stephanie has created. She has built her own security.

One other point about Frank. To some degree, he was hoping and expecting that the sale of his business would be the lion's share of his retirement accumulation. In my many years of working with small businessowners, here is what I can say with experience: sometimes that valuation just never comes to fruition. There have been some instances where the business was actually worth nothing because it was in an outdated industry or it commanded just a fraction of the perceived value for other reasons (poor management, for example). These business owners put their eggs in one basket, and it failed them in terms of delivering the amount they were expecting. Had they used their business as a supplement to their investable accounts in a 401(k), they would have been in a better position. This is an all too common mistake for many small business owners.

Knowledge Is Not So Important

You don't have to know how 401(k) plans work. Or the tax implications. Or dollar cost averaging. Or how mutual funds work. Or target date funds. Or the history of the stock market. You don't have to know anything. You just have to sign up. You just have to enter.

Now, of course, you CAN learn these things if you are so inspired. We live in a world today that information is both abundant and easily accessible. But, it's not necessary. You just don't need to know these things to start on the road to success.

But what you do need to know is what a 401(k) and a retirement plan will do for you. That is what is most critical. It will give you a level and layer of independence in your LATER years, PROPERLY funded. You don't need to be a businessowner or highly paid to be successful. Anyone in the plan has an equal chance of success. Be Stephanie. Be that person that commits to funding their retirement. Make your future your priority, starting today.

Think about an amazing invention from over a century ago, the telephone. In 1876, Alexander Graham Bell was the first not to invent the device but to patent it. It's moved on from it's original design and technology, but the concept is still mind-blowing. We take it for granted these days, but consider just how amazing this device is. We can talk to somebody that his hundreds of miles away in real time. Does our voice travel through the wires and cords we see? How does it work? So few really know HOW a phone works. But what we do know is HOW to use the phone. We know, if we hit the correct number, a call will go through. And if we hit one less number, nothing will happen. We know which end to talk out of and which end to listen. Hence, the is the most *effective means of communication*.

Back to the 401(k). We don't need to know a lot about plans, markets, investing etc., but we know what it can do for us. It gives us the opportunity to build wealth. It offers the true definition of dollar-cost averaging[7] because we are adding monies over regular periods. And so, the 401(k) is the most *effective means of accumulation*.

Do not let "not knowing" delay saving for your long-term future and keep you on the sidelines. You don't know much about how most things in your life work—your car, your computer, your smart phone, your watch—but you know how to use them, you know what they can do for you. Do the same with your 401(k) plan. If you have access to a retirement plan, make it a priority to not only get in but also consider maximizing what you can contribute. Not maximizing to the match that your company may offer, but the limits to what you can contribute (these are different figures). If you are under 50, then you can contribute up to $19,500 (based on 2020 rules), and 50 and over, you can add another $6,500 for the catch-up provision. Those are figures you want to strive for.

Success: Financial Independence

Now let's address success in terms of financial wellbeing, the overarching theme of this book. Although we can assign many different definitions to what that success means or looks like, let's use the generic term, financial independence as the broad goal and narrow it down to having your money and resources to outlive you (i.e., to provide an annual income for the lifestyle you want to live). Let's take a look at how you start the process of getting there.

The critical initial task that puts us on the road to success is that you MUST participate. You need to DEFER some of your own money today. The act of deferring a small piece of todays' resources for the many years of your tomorrows is vital. No longer is anyone else looking out for you like they did in the past. Employers are not interested in securing your long-term financial future (like yesteryear when pensions were more

---

7   Dollar cost averaging does not assure a profit and does not protect against a loss in declining markets. This strategy involves continuous investing; you should consider your financial ability to continue purchases no matter how prices fluctuate.

common). Government programs like Social Security were not designed to be your sole source; they were designed to supplement your income.

This very first step is important for you to know and understand as soon as possible. Because you need to get in and get in now. You need almost every one of your working years, saving and investing to support those later years. Your "attendance" is critical, but the flaw is that it is optional. I see too often, not everyone participates in plans. I rarely see 100% participation in plans.

Success then, financially speaking is rooted in the act of participating, more so than it is in the notion of being smart or picking the "right investment" or earning the most return or making the most money. Of course, those other elements can help but let it be noted that ANYONE can succeed in the financial success game. Success is not limited to high-income earners only as we saw in Frank and Stephanie's stories above.

Going back to a sport analogy, what great athletes do, the common person can't do. Most can't take a handoff and try to escape five 300-pound linemen trying to crush you. Most couldn't put a bat on the ball thrown almost 100 miles per hour. Most couldn't stop today's NBA players from driving on them to the basket. Imagine trying to return the serve of Novak Djokovic? However, almost anyone can enjoy the fruits of financial independence if they follow this near lifetime plan of saving and investing over decades. Their success is relative to their lives, not to others. Meaning, the person that averaged $50,000 of income is not trying to retire on a lifestyle of $200,000. Meaning, each person's independence is about their individuality, their lifestyle, their own choices in life.

So, no matter how much you make, no matter how educated you are, regardless of your socio-economic level, regardless of where you are on your company's totem pole, YOU can achieve financial independence. Anyone can. You can cross that finish line out there that is set up just for you. But YOU have to take action. You have to get in the game.

Participation is the key element. The requirement. Do you see the beauty here? I understand I have repeated this point and will offer it up again because it is not only worth repeating, it is something to really get your head around the sheer beauty of it: success is not for the high-income earners only. This is not an exclusive club that only a few can enter. The expression really hits the mark here: "If it is to be, it is up to me."

Options in Your 401(k)

I want to spend a few moments about your options if you are being offered a chance to enter a 401(k) plan. ENTER as soon as you can. Too often, we seek to minimize what we contribute, so as expressed throughout this book, try to look at the equation as to how you can maximize your contribution. A simple formula is this—the more money you invest, the more money you will have on the back end.

Whatever percent or dollar figure you start with, don't stay for long. Try to get into the habit of either annually or semi-annually, bumping up your contribution a little bit. If you started at 5%, then jump to 6%, then 8% and so on.

With regards to a Roth 401(k) versus contributing towards the traditional deductible option, there is no "right" answer but here are some thoughts. Let's first examine the benefits of each. The traditional deferral gives the individual a deduction upfront, deferred taxes on accumulation, and when you take the monies out, you pay ordinary income taxes (after the age of 59.5). The Roth offers the opposite in that the contribution is an after-tax dollar offering the same no tax on accumulation but at retirement time, the monies come out tax-free.

The general rule is, the younger you are and the less you make, the better a Roth option is for you. As a point of clarification, you can add monies to both the Roth 401(k) and the traditional, up to the deferral limits.

An example of the differences between the two, if you make $50,000 and you want to defer 10% ($5,000), then the traditional method you only pay taxes on $45,000 of current income. For the Roth, you pay taxes on the full $50,000 but the tax benefit is on the back end. The reason this is better for younger people is, as the money compounds, you will have a larger figure at retirement time and that income is tax-free.

I want to end this chapter on one of my favorite quotes about "doing" about being in the game, regardless of the outcome, from President Theodore Roosevelt:

> *It is not the critic who counts; not the man who points out how the strong man stumbles, or where the doer of deeds could have done them better. The credit belongs to the man who is actually in the arena, whose face is marred by dust and sweat and blood; who strives valiantly; who errs, who comes short again and again, because there is no effort without error and shortcoming; but who does actually strive to do the deeds; who knows great enthusiasms, the great devotions; who spends himself in a worthy cause; who at the best knows in the end the triumph of high achievement, and who at the worst, if he fails, at least fails while daring greatly, so that his place shall never be with those cold and timid souls who neither know victory nor defeat.*

Action Items:

- No matter what age you are, you need to start putting money away for your future if you are not already. Get in the game. And if you are in the game, step up your game.
- Take a moment and think about various endeavors in your life and what made you succeed at them and now take a moment to think about what it took to accumulate money in your life. What are these differences?

CHAPTER 9

DIY, Robo or Advisor?

"I measure risk as the probability that we will fail to achieve our goals (of our money outliving us versus us outliving our money) and your professional advisor has dedicated their lives to minimizing that one risk."

Nick Murray

One of the questions each consumer needs to ask and answer for themselves is how will they go about navigating the landscape ahead with concerning their financial future? This chapter will introduce several options and variations of how to go about solving and resolving your financial concerns.

The first option is "do nothing." This is the default option that most take. You don't consciously decide this route so much as give no thought to the overall situation. Typically, this inaction begins when a person is young, having just entered the work force and has no family. Once they start taking responsibility for others, it's harder to ignore. But for those early years, you essentially make money and you spend money. In many cases, you spend equal to or even more than what you make. Of course, this presents both short term and long-term problems. For some, this is a vicious cycle they can't fix, and it becomes a way of life.

The average savings rate in this country is incredibly low, the average retirement account balance is abysmal, and the masses have traveled the road of failure. For many, work is a forever thing and retirement is just a dream. We are often not taught financial responsibility in school or at home, we just fall into our hole from our habits and continue to dig that hole deeper. Spending and consuming are done at will, with little restraint or budgetary concerns. Because of the lack of planning, essentially the situation is akin to driftwood on the ocean, just floating around with no destination or direction.

So, no plan, no strategy, no thought and certainly, no success here. Is this what you want? Is this who you want to be? Hopefully the "do nothing" was a short phase at the early stages of your career and you have started to take advantage of the one critical positive you might have, which is time.

Variations of the Options

Before we discuss several do-something options, let's review some basics. In the United States, the first major stock exchange (the New York Stock and Exchange Board) was created in 1792 on Wall Street. In 1863 it changed its name to the New York Stock Exchange (NYSE). It wasn't until 1924 that the modern-day open-ended mutual fund was started by the fund family MFS and the fund was Massachusetts Investors Trust.[8] That fund is still in existence today.

One can essentially purchase almost any security in a variety of ways today. It can be done through intermediaries like brokers, advisors, firms and of course, yourself. It used to be that the product—being securities

---

8   Mutual funds are sold only by prospectus. Please consider the charges, risks, expenses, and investment objectives carefully before investing. A prospectus containing this and other information about the investment company can be obtained from your financial professional. Read it carefully before you invest or send money.

such as stocks, bonds, and the variations thereof—was the item being purchased. Today, those products and solutions are more commoditized in that consumers now have nearly complete access to these vehicles directly, as well as tremendous information about the companies. They can purchase them on their own. And with information easily accessible and quite abundant, consumers can make more of educated decisions. They can research companies, trends, historical data and even get access to recommendations and suggestions from various sources.

In a sense, this allows the consumer to be their own source and by doing it on their own, they can save the cost of paying someone. But, as we have discovered, there is always a cost; it's just a matter of finding it, understanding the tradeoffs and accepting the differences.

Today, not only are the vehicles accessible for most anyone to acquire but so are some of the tools the industry uses. These could be planning tools, budgeting, asset allocation and aggregation. The trend is that both products and tools have been somewhat commoditized. That begs the question of why would someone want to pay someone for bringing these items to the relationship when they can do it themselves? Well, that, dear reader is a question that is worth exploring.

There is no right solution for all. Simply put, some consumers are best served having a relationship and that relationship oversees some or many of these items. And some consumers are either equipped or comfortable doing pieces themselves or doing it all themselves. As I've shared stories and comparisons all throughout the book, this part of someone's life is no different than other pieces. Some people have the ability and inclination to create and craft "stuff" (for lack of a better technical term) and some people just don't have that skill (or time or desire). Some people enjoy making dinners while others prefer to make reservations. And in each of these, the cost of doing it yourself is often lower. But that is not always accurate, nor is it always the end. Your skill set and abilities might have some limitations or lacking some tools that a professional might have, including experience or access to various tools, so it's not exactly a simple equation of do it yourself. You might save the cost of hiring a professional, but you are unlikely to get the same results that a professional could achieve.

It is certainly incumbent on consumers to play some role in their financial success, whether they take on the various tasks themselves or bring someone else into the process. Let's break down three broad categories that require attention: budgeting/tracking, investing, and planning. This is not to ignore savings at all. Savings are critical but that is something that each consumer can do at their banking institutions. Planning, however, can involve a multitude of items: it could entail education, insurance, retirement, estate and more.

Consumers then need to evaluate these three elements and consider how they will go about solving and resolving them. They can address each themselves, or through some sort of online tool, or they can bring a relationship into the equation. This last option can be done in lieu of the first two, or it could be in addition, meaning that an advisor relationship could be established but the consumer acquires the product offerings on their own. So, you can see, there is no "right" solution. Each consumer must evaluate their own desires, skill sets and more to determine what best suits them.

Do It Yourself

Moving on from the "do nothing" world, here consumers have many options for building on their financial wellbeing themselves. They can take on any combination (or all) of the three branches discussed above: budgeting, investing, and planning on their own.

If this is the road you want to take, there are many tools and sites out there; you don't have to reinvent the wheel. Find the various tools, apps, programs and/or platforms in the marketplace to better assist you in the process. For example, you might consider using a tool to help you manage and budget your expenses. This piece of the puzzle is critically important, especially in the early years of working. We often have a more finite source of money coming in, so being diligent on knowing what comes in and what is going out and when is just so important. If you don't manage or track this, I strongly suggest this is where you start. Write it down on a spreadsheet or search for a budgeting tool.

Investing on your own has become so much easier today than years ago, and fees have dramatically been declining of late. Both access to and affordability have given rise to consumers taking on this task by themselves. Success of DIY investing eventually has to be evaluated, but the mere fact that consumers can get the products and solutions suits some investors. Keep in mind, the product is not necessarily the elixir to cure the problem. Certainly, they are steps in the right direction, but products are just commodities. More on this below.

In rounding out the DIY conversation here, the primary motivation is most likely not wanting to pay cost or fees. Certainly, another motivation is the consumer feels he or she can do the job better than using someone. DIY presents merits to some but for many, this is not what will best serve them. It offers a select few a viable option.

Ask yourself if having a relationship with an advisor would add value. If you feel that relationship offers zero value, consider if it is the relationship that's the problem or the nature of it. Are you talking to the right person? There are many salespeople, agents, and advisors that offer genuine guidance, support, and value in the process. To automatically discard this slice to save some fees or costs might actually cost more in the long run. We've come to glorify the so called zero-commissions society, when that is not necessarily the answer.

Robo Advisor

The robo advisor is the latest trend in the industry making strides with consumers. These are automated investing solutions and services online. Services can be planning, investing, rebalancing, tax optimization, asset allocation and more. Oftentimes, there are low to no account minimums, and fees for these various solutions tend to be lower than using an advisor.

Some platforms will offer some sort of risk questionnaire that will then build a portfolio based on your risk tolerance. Typically, low-cost solutions like index funds or exchange traded funds are the products being represented.[9]

Fees typically will range from 0.25 to 0.50% for robo services, meaning it is roughly a quarter to a half a percent of cost compared to using an advisor. There is tremendous fee compression in the industry across the many lines (investing, account services, planning). The fee for the robo advisor does not include the actual cost of the investment. Each solution will typically have an expense ratio, so passive funds (indexes) often have lower fees than actively managed solutions. Our focus here is not about comparing different fund options. Each (active or passive) offers something of value and exploring those differences will better serve you.

Advisor Relationship

This is an option whereby the consumer hires an individual to help with the services desired. Typically, guidance can come in the form of either

---

[9] Investors should consider carefully information contained in the prospectus, including investment objectives, risks, charges and expenses. Please read the prospectus carefully before investing. Exchange-traded funds do not sell individual shares directly to investors and only issue their shares in large blocks. ETFs are subject to risks similar to those of stocks. Investment returns will fluctuate and are subject to market volatility, so that an investor's shares, when redeemed or sold, may be worth more or less than their original cost.

product and/or process. Beyond guidance, the critical element that more often yields the greatest long-term results is behavioral coaching of the client by the advisor.

Advisors vary in how they invest their clients' monies. Some firms will recommend solutions based on in-house research, while other firms use outside resources. Both offer something of value, depending on the firm you use and its philosophy.

Typical fees for advisors are wide ranging for the various services they offer, and there is also variation in how they charge. And because clients come in different shapes and sizes, this too affects the pricing. For example, the smaller account size means the advisor will tend to charge a higher amount to oversee the investment process. Under $250,000 the range of advisor costs will be from 1% to 1.5%. Some advisors (and firms) will have minimums, so they may not even take on these clients. And that minimum will also vary, so you may see larger advisor firms have minimums at $1,000,000 or even more. As the investable assets increase, you may see that advisor's fee falls, so often it may go below 1%. At several million dollars of investable assets, the fee could range from 0.50% to 0.80% When assets get north of five or ten million, some firms will go to a flat fee.

The above fees are for investing. This does not include planning. Planning is a separate service for some advisors. These are services that are often billed separately and differently (usually a dollar cost for these services). Some will charge a onetime fee to build out the plan and some will then charge an ongoing or annual fee to update and monitor. Fees here range greatly depending on the level of complexity and work being done. For many situations, what a consumer can reasonably expect with regards to a range here is between $1,000 and $5,000 (some planning firms working with high net-worth consumers might have a planning fee range of $10,000–$25,000). Some advisors do not charge at all for planning and include this service in the asset management fee they charge.

The time and support to build out a plan often takes hours, which involves understanding the situation with the client and then drafting the plan. There are a myriad of tools and solutions advisor firms can select from that the industry offers. The more popular plans are now on programs that are dynamic, i.e., as you change a variable, the outcome changes in the presentation. For example, an advisor may build a financial plan for a married couple and, in the first scenario, show the clients retiring at age 64. But in this example, the retirement income might not either last long enough or be large enough for what they want, so using the modeling tool, the advisor can change the retirement age to 70 and see immediately how the retirement plan will be affected. Keep in mind, there many variables in the equation so there is a wide range of outcomes.

The plan will require attention to the many variables at play. Let's take a look at some of the variables in crafting a plan:

- The time you have to your projected retirement
- The years you will have and anticipate in retirement (of course, a great unknown)
- The dollars you can fund your plan with (and where they go)
- The dollars you will need at that next stage in life (retirement)
- The growth rate of the investable dollars (a great unknown but history offers some clues)
- The annual rising cost of goods
- The unforeseen obstacles that happens in life
- Your current and future spending habits
- Your kids and grandkids (if you have) and their needs for help
- Your parents' need for support later in life

- Your ability or inability to keep your income going (could be for health reasons, or redundancy, for example)
- Taxes (going in, accumulating, and coming out)

Some firms, on top of the initial fee to build a plan will also charge an annual fee to monitor and update the plan. This is common as work is being done annually for the client. More often, the first year requires the most work to understand the situation and build out the plan. Subsequent years (updates and reviews) require less time, typically. So, the range of fees here tends to be between 50% and 100% of the first-year cost. So, you might see a firm charge $3,000 to build a plan and then $1,000 a year to update and monitor as an ongoing cost.

As assets grow, the advisor firm might take these planning fees into account, so if investable assets reach $1,000,000 (or more), then the advisor might waive future planning expenses. Again, this varies from firm to firm. Depends on the philosophy of the advising firm, services they offer, tools they use and relationships they seek.

An important point a consumer will want to understand is having an advisor relationship with a fiduciary. What this essentially means is, the advisor is looking out for your best interests. If they do not take on a fiduciary role, then more often, they are commissioned agents. What this means is they can represent products that might be suitable for you. There is a difference between what is suitable for you and what is in your best interest. The highest standard is the fiduciary relationship, so this is one worth establishing.

As an avid golfer, I am in constant pursuit of trying to improve my game. Given the two categories of how to best improve my game—working with a teacher or buying the latest equipment—which route do you think will best improve my game? Having the latest and "greatest" equipment is a commodity but having a teacher improve my technique and guide me, I strongly believe, is a more successful path to better golf. In a similar vain, investment products are a commodity but having a trusted relationship that can guide you will more often lead to better results.

Value Propositions

I'm reminded of a story I read early in my career. Once upon a time, there was a company that manufactured gadgets used by many companies and individuals. Several months after opening its new multi-million assembly plant, the entire operation comes to a standstill. No one could figure out what the problem was. It was costing the company millions of dollars in lost production each day. Finally, after a week, the company hired a consultant. The consultant, after inspecting various pieces of equipment for less than an hour, placed an "X" on one of them. He then told the plant manager to replace it. The problem was solved. The company is back in business. A week later, the plant manager received an invoice from the consultant for $10,000. The plant manager was outraged: $10,000 for less than an hour's work? He fired off a letter asking the consultant for an explanation. About a week later, he received an itemized invoice from the consultant.

	Invoice
For Placing the "X"	$100
For Knowing Where to Place the "X"	$9,900

The moral of the story, clearly, is that most people have problems of which they are not even aware. They need someone with the knowledge and experience to help them identify the problems and then guide them through what needs to be done to help solve those problems.

Varying Solutions Consumers Can Select

For most people, the act of not acting is a way of life. The notion that some can "do it themselves" is acceptable. And then there is a group that wants the highest level of support. This group demands a higher level of guidance. This slice of the consumer market prefers a layer of comfort that comes with a real person guiding them, who is empathetic and listens to their dreams, fears, and concerns; someone who takes the time to understand not just what the client wants but who they are and what legacy they want to build and pass on. That person can bask in their clients' joy and success and can be there in difficult times. The beauty and a significant difference of working with an advisor versus working with a product or online service is continuity. There will be continuity with your advisor that a toll-free support team will not offer. Again, you tend to pay more for that advisor relationship but, clearly, you are getting more.

The consumer needs to determine what layer and level of support and services they want. The industry is moving towards commoditizing the product (investments) and the process (planning). These items can be done or acquired without hiring an individual. If that appeals to you, then that is certainly an option in the marketplace today. Years ago, it was not available.

And for those that want to work with someone, that too is an option that is alive and well. Make no mistake, for many the planner/advisor is the difference maker. Call them whatever you want—guide, shepherd, advisor (or adviser)—the work they perform most likely will result in something different (often times better) than not doing anything. As I expressed prior, there is a cost to having a relationship and there is a cost to not having one. It is for the consumer to evaluate and determine which cost might be more.

Comparison to the Medical Field

Some doctors today work on the concierge philosophy; meaning doctors want a finite number of clients, so they charge them an annual fee so clients have a greater access to the doctor. There are clear benefits and, of course, clear costs. The full scale of benefits might not be something that can be readily measured or seen by the client. For example, maybe the physician is able to spot a problem early because access is more readily available to the client. How can one quantify that benefit?

But what if you didn't have relationship with a doctor, concierge or not? What if you were not feeling well, what options does a consumer have? Of course, do nothing (sound familiar)? Or they could go to an urgent care center or emergency room. If you are sick, you can go to these facilities and they most likely treat a symptom, but they may not catch the bigger issue that is causing the problem. Two years later, if you get sick again and head back to the urgent care center, most likely you will not have the same medical professional attending to your needs. But if you had a personal doctor to go to, then that person will understand your health and history. They might see an underlying problem because they are seeing a bigger picture, they are seeing a history, they are understanding you. A clinic is not able to capture that picture; they are treating a specific ailment and they have a narrower view of the situation.

To Use or Not to Use

The motivation to do it yourself is mostly twofold. Starting out, your situation is rather simple, easy, and limited, such that you can handle the early decision-making. The other reason is fee motivated, in that you don't want to pay a fee for work you feel you can handle. Or pay a lower fee using a platform but not having a personal relationship. Ask yourself this, if hiring an advisor had no cost, would you have an advisor?

As your situation gets more complicated, as you make more money, as your resources expand, does it make more sense to consider removing yourself from the primary role of overseeing your growth and planning? As a starting point, the DIY road has logic, but one must have discipline early on. Eventually, exploring another solution may offer greater upside and provide value.

What You Don't Know Can Hurt You

In your financial world, if you choose to "go it alone", there is a greater chance you would not have maximized your savings and investing … probably wouldn't acquire the appropriate levels of insurance and most likely, would not have drafted a long term retirement plan (meaning most likely, coming up short of your desired intentions). And, a worst case scenario, let's say you didn't acquire the appropriate levels of, say, disability insurance or life insurance, and one of those events occurred … beyond the real life disaster sits the financial wreckage Because you chose to "do it yourself" and didn't know to examine where disability insurance fit in the equation, so you saved $1,000 a year in premiums, but what has it cost you?

I want to reference back to a study brought up in Chapter 7 that is regularly done to compare market returns to investor returns. Markets have thoroughly and consistently beat investors over every 20-year horizon studied. This is because investors tend to bail out of markets when they go down. So, clearly, the value of an advisor relationship can be quantified just in that gap.

Value of an Advisor Study

A study by Vanguard[10] quantified the value of an advisor. The irony here is the very company that administered the study was advocating for investors to go it alone and were the solution for the "do it yourselfers"

---

10 "Putting a Value on Your Value: Quantifying Vanguard Advisor's Alpha," by Donald Bennyhoff, CFA and Francis Kinniry Jr, CFA

for years. Yet, in their study, they determined that the value of an advisor equals about 3% per year. Feel free to google that study to read more, "Quantifying Your Value to Clients."

The article goes on to say that value is driven in a relationship through services such as wealth management and behavioral coaching. In addition, other areas of value can be driven in estate planning, succession planning, advice on various insurances, as well as charitable giving. The article also comments that those working with advisors tend to have "greater peace of mind, larger account balances, and a better understanding that some portfolio risks may have been reduced."

It won't be because the advisor necessarily gave you a better solution in terms of an investment. The end product you invest in might be the same had you gone down the road on your own or using a robo advisor. But, the focus here is less about the commodity of the product and more about their inclination to prevent you, the consumer, from making one of a host of mistakes (that each has a price tag). These pitfalls could be:

- Not starting soon enough
- Not funding long term plans with enough
- Acting/reacting to market dips and drops
- Acting/reacting to media and financial journalism
- Over-diversified
- Under-diversified
- Timing the market
- Unaware of the available options (selecting one that doesn't fully serve the situation)
- Confusing risk and volatility
- Not understanding the real issue at hand
- Thinking the cost of a solution is the problem when it is the potential solution

- Refusing to seek guidance and help when appropriate
- Tax implications
- Wrong amount and use of insurance products
- Not saving enough, not having savings at all
- Not having a long-term plan of action
- Little or no continuity

Any one of these could be damaging, but several of these could be devastating. And the good work by those professionals in the business will more often address and pay attention to every single one of these and more. And because of this, they will (again, more often) offer a value proposition beyond what the relationship costs. Meaning, they should bring to the table an appreciative difference in actions, decision-making and path, relative to what they charge.

Another Study

There was another study in 2014, which revealed something interesting. The article starts with: "If you want good investment performance, forget you have an account." They studied accounts and found that the accounts that did the best over a particular stretch were from clients that DIED. Yes, from clients who died because they didn't move their portfolio around or panic and get out.

Interesting that two of the larger money managers that promote the "do it yourself" model came to these conclusions. The value of an advisor can be beneficial in helping build and protect wealth.

Keep in mind, that no advisor relationship can relieve you of the responsibility for you and your family's financial independence, but a plan and said planner can remove much of the anxiety, offer confidence, and provide a resource. For many, that is worth the price of admission.

You are buying the planner more than the plan or a product. And a quality relationship will be worth untold multiples of what it costs.

You may want to make a note of what is not the advisor's responsibility: it is not for the advisor to be "right" about markets. They are not prognosticators or predictors of market movement, or experts in when an investor should get in or get out. That is a fools' game. They can't predict which fund, investment or sector of the marketplace will outperform; that is not their job. Products are the commodities they use to get you from point A to point B, but products are not the focal point. More often, the plan and destination are the focus (where you stand relative to your customized goals, your individual situation), not whether your fund outperformed some index.

Between the studies done by these organizations, there is a clear message that the value of an advisor relationship may outweigh the fee they charge most of the time. If I use the industry norm of 1% fee for asset management to bring on board an individual advisor relationship, these studies each show the consumer will more than make up that difference. This is where value intersects with advisor.

How to Know if Planning Is Important

The following questions will help determine if planning is important to you. If you don't readily know these answers, then the process and building of a plan will address these very issues:

- Do you know what your financial assets are?
- What are you currently doing with regards to your savings, protection and investing strategies?
- Taking into account your current list of assets and resources AND what you are currently doing (both of the above), do you have any idea where this will take you in terms of your goals?
- Based on your current lifestyle, do you know where you "need to be" or "want to be" for retirement? (Keep in mind, this is

different from the current road you are on – where you want to be and where you are potentially ending up might be two different locations).

- Is there a gap between where you are going and where you would like to be?
- Do you have a trusted relationship assisting in the journey, offering guidance and support, presenting ideas, monitoring along the way, adjusting strategies as life presents changes?
- Is there a layer of organization, understanding, and tracking taking place?

The first two questions, I suspect you may know, but would you like to know the answers to the other questions? This is the essence of planning. Investing and the process of planning are a constant and ongoing element, the work done requires updates and modifications. Setting up a plan and a process is the start but not the end.

As a consumer, you will want to ask, to better understand what the advisor does and how they work. Here are a few questions you may want to ask them when you interview them:

- How do they work? Talk about the tools and process they use.
- Are they independent or do they have an "allegiance" or loyalty to a company or product?
- How are they compensated?
- What can you expect in the relationship?
- How often will you meet and talk (and how often will they reach out via emails and such)?
- Who do they typically do work for (ideal client)?
- What support do they have?
- What are their philosophies about money, investing, and retirement?

Keep in mind as you are interviewing them that they are also interviewing you. They probably want to make sure you are a fit for them and their firm.

Wrapping Up

As you can see, there are many choices for solving support for your financial needs. There are no "right answers" that solves for all. There is a right solution for you and, candidly, it might not be the first one you start with. You might find that starting on your own leads you to realizing the importance of a relationship. You might also run the opposite direction, in that you started with someone but the relationship failed, so you felt it was within your means to change to a self-help option. Whatever your path, keep asking questions. Answers tend to follow and from that, a clearer path will present itself.

Action Items:

- If you have not worked with an advisor before, consider where one might be able to add value. Schedule a meeting with one to see how they work, what they would do, and if it feels right. If after meeting with one it doesn't feel right, consider interviewing another. The key element in the relationship should be the process they drive, not the products they offer. Are they building a plan to help you get to financial independence?

- Take inventory. Whether you decide to bring someone onboard to help or not, see where you are, what you are spending, what money is coming in and what are you putting forth to secure your long-term future. If you are paying more for cable TV or your cell phone bill than you are setting aside for your future self, you need to assess your priorities and strongly consider altering some of your current expenses to boost your contributions to long term investing.

CHAPTER 10

Why We Work

"I can't change the direction of the wind, but I can adjust my sails to always reach my destination."

Jimmy Dean

There is the well-known expression that money doesn't buy happiness. But it is also true that having no money doesn't make people happy, because worry and fear and the need to keep working long after you want to retire is not a recipe for joy. Money allows one to live differently. To do things, to travel, to give, to indulge, to engage, to explore, to try, and play a part in many things. Money is a medium of exchange to open doors.

I have seen some people for whom work is everything and they have little or nothing beyond their work, but I have also met people whose interests and hobbies and passions in life coexist with their professional lives. For some, work defines us. And although I don't want to pass judgment on that grouping, I want you to consider why you work, and why you will want to save, protect and invest over the course of your life. Besides comfort, what's it all for?

My "why" for working is to make a difference in my clients' lives, to make an impact, to be part of their success story. When a client acknowledges a positive difference in their lives, it fuels me. And while I do want work to define some parts of me, I don't want to be exclusively defined by the role I play. I have passions outside of my occupation, and that is what I'm wanting to point out here for you by sharing some relationships I have come across over my years to showcase people who have attained a work-life balance.

Jeff

Although Jeff, my doctor, is not one of my clients, he is someone I have gotten to know over the many years of my adult life and he's in that category of people I hold in high regard. He's dedicated to his role as a physician and always takes the time for his patients and never makes me feel like a number. He is very successful at his craft, but beyond that, he's an excellent photographer, plays the drums, is a good golfer, and to top it off, a wonderful family man—an involved husband, father and grandfather.

Artie

Artie, one of my clients, was climbing Mount Kilimanjaro as I started writing this book. He's never climbed a mountain, but he's taken this challenge and decided to be with his daughter and push himself. He's been training the last six months, preparing his body and mind for the task. I just love that he's reached a certain stage of life, worked hard to accumulate dollars to step aside from work , is young and healthy enough to engage in something like this, and decided, "I'm going to do this while I can."

Money didn't buy this happiness, but it sure paved the way to allow Artie to do this. Artie isn't letting life dictate to him; he's earned this right to be himself and do what brings him joy because of the sound financial decisions he's made (prior to me) for years. He's now taking control of this next stage of life by living out his desires. I won't say "dreams" because it's not always something we dream or think about. Sometimes, we want to try something or do something spontaneously, but we don't always have flexibility to respond to something unexpected.

Jenn

When we had a garden built in our back yard a few years ago, my wife, Jenn, realized it was her happy place. She literally gets to eat the fruits of her labor. We expanded it over the years, and she's learned from the mistakes she made her first season of planting. There are no prizes besides her end results. There are no finish lines, and no one is offering her money for her results. You don't have to be good or even great at something. You just have to enjoy it. It doesn't have to be competitive or measurable. She does this for herself and for the delayed satisfaction of planting seeds, seeing them grow, watching a fruit or vegetable blossom, and weeks later picking it and eating it. But it's the passion she has. She has developed a strong work ethic and a tremendous reputation as an SAT tutor, but she's come to learn there are other parts of who she is.

Gary

A long-standing client and close friend of mine, Gary, is another person that it's been really cool to see grow over the years. It's the success of his physical therapy practice that has ultimately allowed him to pursue his passions. He was diligent about saving, protecting, and investing long term. He was prudent about choices in life, raising three beautiful girls and supporting them and their education. And over decades of doing this, along with the growth of the practice, this has allowed him to venture into one of his passions, fishing. And now he spends many of his off days on the waters, his happy place.

Smitty

Another relationship I hold in high esteem is a guy I play golf with, Smitty. On top of being a veteran, a graduate of West Point, a businessowner, and one hell of a golfer, he's an artist (painting and sculpture), a war historian, and an author. His interests outside his occupation are vast and deep, and he excels at everything he does.

Ken and Beth

Lastly, Ken and Beth have a deep passion of living a life of mental and physical excellence. They take care of themselves like few others I know and are supportive of their boys as involved parents. Ken is a successful attorney as a partner in a large law firm and Beth has paved her way as personal coach and motivator. Being successful didn't define them. It just allowed them the pathway to their passions of living life to their fullest

The piles of money these people have don't necessarily make them happy; it's what they can do with that security. It's what it allows them to venture and explore what makes them happy. I only shared a few to highlight the diversity of passions. Find your why. Discover what it is for you. Consider the joys of being a part time pastry chef (please invite me over), or like Jeff and being a photographer, or learning magic, or an instrument, or collecting something, or spending time in the garden. What are your passions besides work? What do you love doing? Where do you feel good? What is your happy place? What things in life can you engage in, learn, develop a skill in, immerse yourself? If you don't have a why, then I strongly encourage you to think about it..

Then explore further. What is it you want to do, accomplish, try? I implore you to explore. Step away and be reflective on this topic. You can have passions while raising kids and excelling at your job. There are plenty of days and hours in the year that you don't need to think, breathe and engage in work.

Don't wait until you are done working to figure this out. Give it thought now. Maybe it is something that is competitive (running a race or marathon) or a skill you want to learn (an instrument, baking, cheesemaking). It doesn't have to cost a lot. Of course, some hobbies are more expensive than others, but you don't have to buy a boat to enjoy fishing. You don't have to join a club to learn how to play golf. Pickleball (a cross between tennis, table tennis and badminton) is one of the fastest growing sports and a paddle will cost about $100 and lessons are very reasonable. It's something Jenn and I have recently taken up together.

Strike a balance. Explore and find something you enjoy. But doing something is the key. Don't wait for "retirement" to do this. By the time you have reached that later stage of life, you might not have the health to start something new, so start thinking about what makes you happy. What is the point of having gold if you can't generate joy? The financial independence is not necessarily the end: think about what it will allow you to do leading up to and within those later stages? Is there a mountain out there for you to climb? Is there a challenge out there waiting for you to step up? Is there a passion inside of you bursting to come out?

Action Items:

- Think about your passions and joys. Do you engage in them enough? Do you spend enough time in your happy places?
- Have you struck a balance between working hard and life outside of work? The exception here is when you are young when you have to spend a larger amount of time getting established, working off excess debt, and possibly taking a second job to make ends meet, then there are times in life that "doing what you have to do" is necessary. But at some point, there must be some relief and release.

- Think about your peers, friends or family who are closer to retirement. Can you tell which ones have a hobby, play an instrument, have a craft, do some sort of art, and which ones seem to have little outside of their work? Consider how this affects our perception of them. Do you aspire to be them? Do you respect them?

CHAPTER 11

Story Time and Do's and Don'ts

"If you don't know where you are going, you might not get there."

Yogi Berra

You have reached the last chapter and we've covered a lot. I want to use these last few pages together to wrap up some thoughts, review some points, and remind you of tasks that need attention. It is my hope that you see the path a bit more clearly to work on your blueprint, so you have greener pastures in your golden years.

Make small changes, find a few nuggets within these pages, and alter some of your behavior. The direction you head in is more critical than the speed. Eventually, you can pick up the speed, and reverse the bad habits, to build your financial independence. Focus on spending less, saving more, better investing habits, thinking long term, keeping debt in check … and over a few years, step up these actions. Invest more, save more, reduce debt faster: this is what I'm referring to with speed. This is your life, this is your future, build it accordingly to what your desires are, what you are dreaming of.

The thing with success is that YOU must take the initiative. You have to take responsibility for the action. It will not grab you and force you to do or act. Other than your parents pushing you, there is no one out there suggesting you study, be better, do more. There is an element of motivation, being a self-starter and recognizing who takes the initiative. You.

Be Realistic

In filling your "pool of money," just make sure you are in touch with reality in terms of adding water to your hole in the ground. You can't use an eye dropper or even a glass of water. That would just be lunacy to fill your pool. Even a bucket of water every so often wouldn't get the job done. There must be a flow; there must be some regularity.

You will have to find consistent dollars over time to fund your long-term accumulation goal. You will have to make a greater commitment, a greater sacrifice, over the years ... otherwise, the sacrifice you will be forced into is working all your living years (or living an undesired lifestyle).

There is an expression that can be used in many endeavors in life: "You get out what you put in." Those who practice (for example, in a sports endeavor) often see better results. Those who study often see better grades. Those who work out are often in better health. And those that fund their long-term accumulation have greater resources. With creating your own wealth, the fact is that if you don't set aside dollars over long periods that accumulate and compound, then you will never magically have wealth (the exceptions being inheritance or lottery). But for the majority of people that won't inherit enough to change their lives or win a big payout, it is rather simple: we must take matters into our own hands. Not easy, but logical and doable.

One Thing That Won't Happen

Don't worry about overfunding it. No one ever said, when they hit retirement: "Oh my goodness, we have too much money ... what are we ever going to do with all this money? We saved too much." So, push your limits, find your balance, and be committed.

Do's and Don'ts

A summary of key points from the book.

- **Do** start. Start with looking at your situation, start with what needs attention the most, start with saving more, spending less, increasing your retirement contribution, finding a "game" to play to squirrel a few extra dollars away here and there. Sometimes that is the hardest part, but inertia is powerful, so start. Small is okay. But small is not okay forever; you need to step up at some point.

- **Do** seek help and guidance. We use professionals in many facets of our lives, so having someone to guide us through the maze will not be a cost factor but a value-added item. At the very least, explore where someone can add value.

- **Do** save. Not always popular, but some liquidity is a good thing. Set up separate accounts that address different issues and stay disciplined in keeping them separate.

- **Do** implement a hoarding policy on cash to see what you can "sock away" … find a game to play to put a few bills away over time as described in an earlier chapter and see what comes. Create your own security and comfort.

- **Don't** overestimate your ability to solve problems, to recognize your own danger, to pull yourself out of a mess.

- **Don't** heed financial journalism's guidance as the be all and end all. Recognize their goal and their audience and apply perspective. One can literally find an article, blog, ad every single day (without even trying) that gives conflicting information to your long-term strategy or facts that really don't apply to your situation. Learn to discard it … better yet, train yourself to not even engage it if you can.

- **Don't** fall into the trap that you may spend less in retirement. You might. But you might not. You might actually spend more, and mark my words: if you had the resources to not worry about money, you would do things differently. You would take family vacations; you might help grandchildren with their education. You might consider living differently then had you imagined leading up to your retirement.
- **Don't** look at a long-term problem and solve it with a short-term thinking. When you are stuck in a traffic jam, don't get out of your car, abandon it and start walking to your destination.
- **Don't** take the mentality that you have decades until retirement and not put forth effort and resources to save. Start immediately. **Don't** succumb to the thinking that you will start next year.
- **Don't** overanalyze. Keep in mind that action (even if that action isn't perfect or 100% right) trumps inaction. Doing nothing is actually going backwards.
- **Don't** dig your hole faster than your ability to fill it. Keep debt at a manageable level.
- **Don't** cash-in old/prior retirement plans as you change jobs if you don't really have to. Sometimes, life gets in the way and we have to make decisions contrary to what is best long term, but understand that and be diligent and determined the next few years to play catch up.
- **Don't** do nothing if that first year of a new job if you have a 1 year wait to enter a retirement plan, add or open an IRA.
- **Don't** pick a deferral amount and never increase it. Bump it up annually, even a small increment. Go from 5% to 6% to 8% … keep going. Work to contributing the maximum amount that plan rules allow.

- **Don't** max out a deferral on a 401(k) up to the company match. **Do** contribute a higher percentage if you can and if you can't come back next year and bump it up.
- **Don't** react to market gyrations. Markets rise and they fall. Stick to a plan and being emotional is not a plan. It's a reaction that is often devastating to your long-term plans.

Blue, Green, and Gold

Consider drafting a **blueprint** for your financial life (or having an independent person help you). This is something that requires ongoing work. There is no end but there is a beginning. That blueprint will lead to those **greener pastures**. A better life. Isn't that what we all want? More security, greater freedom, allows us to do what we want, have the things in life we desire, support family members if we choose, give to organizations to the amount we want, make an impact on others. And we can do this in those **golden years** of our life. We get to reap the rewards of our hard work. We get to eat the fruits of those trees that we planted decades ago. And the beauty is, those fruits just keep coming back if we planted enough of them. Having gold in those golden years is … well, pretty nice. At the other end of the rainbow is a pot of gold. It will take time, effort, diligence, patience and probably some guidance to fill that pot.

And the beauty is, as expressed earlier, anyone can do this. This is open season for anyone that is motivated, disciplined and driven.

Good luck. Thank you for allowing me to share my stories with you. Thank you for spending one of the greatest commodities you possess with me, your time. I hope you were able to garner a few nuggets in these pages that will help you build and fill your pool.

Feel free to email me if you got something positive from these pages, I welcome hearing from you. It fuels me to know I might have made a difference.

APPENDIX

Action Items

- It is my suggestion that you have a note pad or highlighter as you read and when something is stated that hits home, jot it down. Reflect upon your situation and think about what changes you can make.
- Think about your current retirement plan. Are you on the proper path? Is your trajectory one you are proud of or does it need attention?
- How many of the categories described have you encountered in your life?
- How many can you put in your past—can you work to eliminate?
- Which ones are the top three you need to eliminate in your life?
- Over the next three months, gather a few pieces on the internet that offer market related guidance and build a small collection to reference back. Build your own file to then look back and see how much turned out to be detrimental to your long-term portfolio and what that offered sound guidance. This will allow you to see firsthand, that not everything posted or written is the truth or its advice that is best serving you specifically.

- Look up what the Dow Jones and the S&P 500 indexes were the year you were born. And of course, look up where it is today. And take a moment to bask in how our market has performed in those years. Keep in mind, what you are seeing is only the price movement of the index, not the dividend it has paid, so you'll need to take that into account (for example, the S&P has averaged about 2% dividend per year). Even with the so-called bear markets.

- The real action item is to remove yourself from reading and listening to the financial pornography. If you can do that, then I strongly believe you will be better off in the long run.

- Consider for a moment in our last really deep market "crash" (2007–2008), what if you did the opposite of what these articles suggested, and instead of getting out, you doubled down and got in with more money? If you could, would you have invested more money then? Even at the peak, would you have?

- You must understand your time horizon. What is your estimate of years you have to work before retirement? For example, if you are 42 and you want to retire at 66, then you have 24 years to accumulate money.

- Understand from a compounding point of view what could you save/invest and at some reasonable growth rate and calculate what that will grow to. With that figure, ask yourself if it is a figure you could comfortable, reasonably retire on.

- If the answer is no or not even close, then you will need to take a hard look at extending the time horizon, finding ways to reduce current consumption/spending so you can increase annual contributions. Remember, this is your life, your lifestyle in those later years, so addressing this is all about you.

- Take an inventory of your overall insurance and discuss with an independent advisor to see where, if at all, there are gaps and shortages.
- For life insurance, think through what happens if a death occurs. Who will be financially affected and can they support themselves? Then explore what that cost would be to close those gaps. Compare that premium cost to their shortage.
- Before rejecting the idea of both disability insurance and LTC, seek to find someone or several who have experienced the need for this coverage and see what they have to say. Most likely, you will get the core, painful truth about mistakes they made and what they would have done differently.
- Determine what your Pure Savings and Put & Take account levels are. Then consider what are your monthly expenses? Start with three months' expense in the Pure Savings. For the time being, start with between $2,000 and $3,000 of P & T. Determine how long it will take to get to those levels.
- When you have those two accounts set up (they don't have to be fully funded but established), open a "house / vacation" account. Start to get that savings account going. The house account can be for someone who doesn't yet own but wants to buy something, or it can be for someone who owns but is preparing for that next upgrade.
- Start your $5 bill game. Put a cup in your closet and during the course of your week, pull out the $5 bills you get and fill the cup. Watch it grow.
- Take a look back at your investing history and make note of what you did, when you did it and why. Were those actions beneficial in the long run or were they detrimental to your long-term growth? Did you stop investing in the last draw down? Or did you panic and sell holdings?

- Take note of where investing is in your priorities. Have you flatlined in terms of how much you have been investing the last 5, 10 or even 20 years? Have you spent more on other items but not your retirement nest egg? Make it a greater priority. Explore how you can max out in your retirement plan to the limit of what you can invest in the plan.

- Talk to some family members willing to share what they did about saving and investing and why. Maybe this is a moment that you can learn from someone else's mistakes. This is not for you to point out what they did wrong but for you to see in "real life" situations, what could have been different for your parents or grandparents. Gaining perspective might alter your path. Did they save enough? Did they save at all? What would they have done differently? What experience did they have in equity markets? Maybe there are nuggets there for the taking, but it might not be in what they did; it might be more in what they didn't do, and they might not realize it.

- No matter what age you are, you need to start putting money away for your future if you are not already. Get in the game. And if you are in the game, step up your game.

- Take a moment and think about various endeavors in your life and what made you succeed at them, and now take a moment to think about what it took to accumulate money in your life. What are these differences?

- If you have not worked with an advisor, explore where one might be able to add value. Schedule a meeting with one to see how they work, what they would do and if it feels right. If after meeting with one, it doesn't feel right, consider interviewing another. The key element in the relationship should be the process they drive, not the products they offer. Are they building a plan to help you get to financial independence?

- Take inventory. Whether you decide to bring someone onboard to help or not, see where you are, what you are spending, what monies are coming in and what are you putting forth to your long-term future. If you are paying more for cable TV or your cell phone bill than you are to your future self, assess your priorities and strongly consider altering some of your current expenses to boost your contributions to long-term investing.
- Think about your passions and joys. Do you engage in them enough? Do you spend enough time in your happy places?
- Have you struck a balance between working hard and life outside of work? The exception here is when you are young when you have to spend a larger amount of time getting established, working off excess debt, and possibly taking a second job to make ends meet, then there are times in life that "doing what you have to do" is necessary. But at some point, there must be some relief and release.
- Think about your peers, friends or family who are closer to retirement. Can you tell which ones have a hobby, play an instrument, have a craft, do some sort of art, and which ones seem to have little outside of their work? Consider how this affects our perception of them. Do you aspire to be them? Do you respect them?

www.ingramcontent.com/pod-product-compliance
Lightning Source LLC
Chambersburg PA
CBHW070047230426
43661CB00005B/793